RED BOOK

of

SUPER FAST SPOKEN ENGLISH

DHARMENDRA SIR

Published By

Invincible Publishers

Published by

Invincible Publishers
201A, SAS Tower, Sector 38, Gurugram – 122003
Phone: +91-124-4034247, +91 9599066061
www.invinciblepublishers.com

Sales: Office No. 4760-61/23 Basement, Pratap Street,
Ansari Road Daryaganj, New Delhi. 110002
Phone: +91-11-40198405
Email: invinciblepublishers@gmail.com

First edition – 2023

ISBN: 978-93-94200-98-2

Content

Units

Unit-1 Spoken and Personality

(बोलचाल और व्यक्तित्व)

There are 'four' important rules which every student as to follow with in the coaching hours.

(i) Don't speak even a single word of hindi, try to speak english if you are present here or anywhere.

(ii) Unity rule : Unity creates the environment.

(iii) Respect to your teacher.

(iv) Wishing rule.

Wishing Time

Night **Day**

(a) 12 : 01 second to 11 : 59 minutes (day)
(a.m. – anti meridiem)

(b) 12 : 01 second to 11: 59 minute
(p.m.-post meridiem)

First Meeting

Night **Day**

(a) 12 : 01 a.m. to 11 : 59 a.m. → Good Morning.

(b) 12 : 01 p.m. to 3 : 59 a.m. → Good Afternoon.

(c) 4 : 01 p.m. to 11 : 59 p.m. → Good Evening.

Last Meeting

Night **Day**

(a) 12:01 a.m. to 6:00 a.m. → Good day or have a nice day.

(b) 6:01 p.m. to 11:59 p.m. → Good night or have a sweet dream.

English Communication

1. English is not a language rather it is the communication.

Que. What is communication?

Ans : it is the link cum official language.

Que. Why is english communication

Ans : It is adapted language.

How will you learn English

(i) You must have a good get up.
(ii) You have to break your hesitation
(iii) You have to speak english to english.
(iv) You have to have the deep knowledge regarding the chapter.
(v) You have to have self confidence.
(vi) You have to increase your interest and develop your environment.

These items are linked to each other, which are very much important for speaking english.

- Your hard labour
- Home works (over target till 3 months)
- Conversation → Event
- Group discussion → on paper G.D.
- Seminar and debate context
- Role play

Verb

- It is the basics foundation of english communication.
- If you know the use of verb well, you can speak correct and fluent english in a short span of time.

There are two types of verb – (i) Main verb (ii) Helping verb

If you want correct and fluent english you have to command on sentence.

- We have to make a meaningful and senseful sentence, four factors are needed.

Factor A – Subject :

There are many subject but we have to use six subject – I, You, We, They, He, She.

Factor B – Helping verb

There are fifteen important helping verb series of the helping verb.

is, am, are, has, have, do, does	← Used in present time
was, were, had, did, used to	← Used for past time
Will have, will be, will	← Used for future time

Factor C – Main Verb

There are five types of main verb – V^1, V^2, V^3, V^4 and V^5.

Factor D – Object

Without object we can't make the meaningful and senseful sentence, because it is the mirror of the sentence.

Structure : S + Is/are/am/ + V^4 + Object.

Ex.

(1) I am writing a letter
(Positive sentence) — **Art of Answer**

(2) I am not writing a letter
(Negative sentence) — **Art of Answer**

(3) Am I writing a letter
(Positive question)

(4) Am I not writing a letter
(Negative question)

(5) When am I writing a letter
(Question with 'WH')

(6) Why am I not writing a letter
(Question with 'WH' Negative)

(3)–(6): **Art of Question**

In spoken

I	changed	You
You	changed	I
He	changed	he
She	changed	she

Practice with these Subjects

I	You	He	They	He	She
1 × 6	1 × 6	1 × 6	1 × 6	1 × 6	1 × 6
4 × 6	4 × 6	4 × 6	4 × 6	4 × 6	4 × 6
10 × 6	10 × 6	10 × 6	10 × 6	10 × 6	10 × 6

Personality

It is the internal and external characteristics of a person.

Internal → 80 to 90%

1. Internal characteristics of

Mind and **Body**
↓ ↓
(knowledge) (pure heart)

2. **External 10 to 20%**

(i) Confidence
(ii) Outlook
(iii) Dress makeup
(iv) Activity.

Types of Personality

(i) Egoist
(ii) Egotist
(iii) Introvert
(iv) Extrovert
(v) Ambivert
(vi) Ascetic
(vii) Altruist

(i) Egoist (अहंवादी) → Egoism (स्वार्थी) : The Person who makes every decision on one question that is what is my benefit in it.
Self welfare, Self advancement.
Conclusion – it is a bad personality.

(ii) Egotist (डींग मारना, शेखी बघारना) :
A person who think that they are better than other people and who think and talk too much about himself.
Conclusion : It is a bad personality.

(iii) Introvert

(i) He is generally shy.
(ii) He may be intelligent.
(iii) He has a confusing personality.
(iv) Unwanted self analysis.
(v) He prefers solitude than groups.

↓

Pessimistic (निराशावादी) approach

↓

Inferiority complex

(हीन भावना)

"inferiority complex" is a term for describing chronic feelings of inadequacy and insecurity.

(iv) Extrovert

(i) He is not shy.
(ii) He may be intelligent.
(iii) He is not confused personality.
(iv) He is a bold personality.

Conclusion : It is a good personality.

(v) Ambivert (उभयमुखी)

Ambi + Verto
↓ ↓ → Intro + Extro
Both Turn (–) + (–)
= + Personality

Conclusion : It is a super personality.

(vi) Altruist (परोपकारी)

One who is interested in the welfare of himself as well as the welfare of others.
He gives priority to the welfare of others.

(vii) Ascetic (तपस्वी)

He has the character of a saint or hermit.
He does not keep interest in worldly pleasure.

Five Golden Skills (पाँच स्वर्णिम कौशल)

1. Praise people – Honey attracts more than vinegar.

लोगों की प्रशंसा करें – शहद, सिरके से ज्यादा अच्छा लगता है।

Always have a good thing to say about the person you meet. Honey attracts more than vinegar. Praise people. Make them feel happy.

They will make you feel happy.

2. Handle objection (आपत्तियों को दूर करें)

Let them see that you respect and understand what they are saying, but that you are confident and can help them anyway.

Never argue with the person when he is expressing his objection.

Never intersect. Never be defensive or insulting.

3. Thank people (लोगों का शुक्रिया अदा कीजिए)

It is a good manners to say "thank you" Let the other person know that you appreciate what they have done. People like being thanked and like the people who show their gratefulness.

4. Smile (मधुर मुस्कान)

Smile naturally and sincerely. Don't grin artificially but smile enough to show that you are interested in the person. Look at the person to whom you are talking.

Expression that you wear on your face make a much greater impact than the clothes you wear.

Presentable (मोहक अंदाज)

There is no "dress for success." You should be neat and clean and well groomed. hair should be short, preferably clean shave.

Don't be over-dressed but certainly don't be under dressed. You should not feel out of place, have a good manner.

- To look up and not down.
- To look forward and not back.
- To look out and not in.

Body Language

Body Language

1. Theoretical | **2. Practical**

Body Language : Body language, which plays a significant role in communication, refers to all external stimulus, that is physical appearance and personality. Our body always conveys a meaning of some kind even if we are not conscious of it. We communicate not only through words but also through our whole body.

Therefore, essential to pay attention to your body language in fact, the control of the body movements even before your speak is imperative.

Theoretical	**Practical**
1. Personal appearance	1. Sitting Position
2. Posture – pose - (दिखावा)	2. Facial expression
3. Gesture – (संकेत, चेष्टा)	3. How to stand
4. Eye contact	4. Eye contact
	5. Hand expression
	6. Experience

(1) Personal Appearance :

- Personal appearance is a significant non-verbal clue to your personality.
- **Physical appearance :** Your physique general attractiveness, personal hygiene, body odour, hair style, skin tone etc.
- When you make a public appearance, your dress should be suitable for the occasion and of course neat and clean and attractive.
- The physical presence is also influenced by certain abstract qualities such as self-confidence and self-knowledge.
- A conscious cultivation of these qualities would increase your speaking power.

(2) Posture :

- Posture is the way you conduct yourself when you face an audience. Don't play with your bunch of keys or coins or buttons. When you are invited to speak;
- Look at the entire audience pause for a while and then start speaking. After you have finished speaking, go back to your seat with the same confidence as you come to the podium.

(3) Gesture (संकेत)

- A gesture is the movement of head, arms or hand to illustrate or reinforce what on says.
- It increases the value of spoken words and exercises a deeper impact upon listeners. In fact, it is difficult to speak without using gesture.
- There are a few consideration which you should bear in mind while speaking in puplic.
  - **First** – let, there be a proper integration of the hand movement with the verbal material.
  - **Last** – there is a need for controlling gestures so that they suit the occasion and the audience.

(4) Eye contact :

- Of the five sense organs, the eyes are the most expressive. They act as the window of the mind. It can express elemental passions as well as varying moods of person.
- Looking at the audience is not at all. You should know how to look at them.
- Remember, eye contact reveals the speaker's personality and helps him overcome his self confidence.

Practical

1. **Sitting postion :** Don't shake your leg when you are in chair.
2. **Facial expression :** Always keep your facial expressions positive.
3. **How to stand :** You don't try to stand on one foot and don't shake your legs.
4. **Eye contact :** You watch your listeners carefully. Don't see 'hither and thither'.
5. **Hand expression :** Don't shake your hand meaninglessly. First and formost rule is → what type of matter you are going to speak.

Express Yourself

- I would like to tell you something about myself
- Let me tell you something about myself
- I am going to/gonna tell you something about myself
- As far as I am concerned
- I want to/wanna tell you something about myself

My name is ....I was born and brought up (जन्म और पालन-पोषण) in Delhi now I am living at ....I am a straight forward and sophisticated person. I have always been positive attitude towards everyone

About my qualification at present I am doing graduation from Delhi University prior to it I did my schooling from C.B.S.E board of Delhi. My favorite subject is English.

Let me tell you about my family background. I belong to a middle class family. My father is in govt. /pvt sector and my mother is a homemaker. I have ......siblings.

My hobbies include listening to music and meeting knowledgeable people.

My aim is to become.......

Thank you

It is all about my self

Now, prepare your introduction by yourself

Some important statement

- I would like to .... मैं चाहूँगा ....
- Let me tell you about........... मैं आप को .... बारे में बताता हूँ।
- I am going to/gonna................. मैं .... गा, गे, गी
- As far as (xyz) is/are concerned जहाँ तक की .... का सवाल है।
- I want to/wanna .... मैं .... चाहता हूँ।

Verb to be

Positive : Subject + is/am/are + other words.
Negative : Subject + is/am/are + not + other words.
Interrogative : Is/am/are + Subject + other words?
Negative : Is/am/are + Subject + not + other words?
Wh : Wh. + is/am/are + Subject + other words?
Wh. Negative : Wh. + is/am/are + Subject + not + other words?

Is / am / are

ID. – है, हूँ, होता है, होती है, होते हैं, रहता है, रहती है, रहते हैं

He, She, It, Mohan → **is**

We, You, They, Boys → are

I —— am

For example

1. तुम पागल हो — You are mad.
2. तुम पागल नहीं हो — Yoy are not mad.
3. क्या तुम पागल हो — Are you mad?
4. क्या तुम पागल नहीं हो — Are you not mad?
5. तुम पागल क्यों हो — Why are you mad?
6. तुम पागल क्यों नहीं हो — Why are you not mad?

Wh. Family

1. What – क्या
2. Whose – जिसका/किसका
3. How – कैसे
4. Why – क्यों
5. Where – कहाँ
6. When – जब
7. Which – कौन-सा/कौन सी
8. Who – कौन

Exercise

1. वह मेरा मुँह बोला भाई है। ....
2. वह मेरा दुश्मन नहीं है। ....
3. यह कार किसकी है? ....
4. क्या आप घर पर हो? ....
5. आप उदास क्यों हैं? ....
6. क्या आप दलाल हैं? ....

7. क्या आपका दोस्त आवारा है? ....
8. क्या वे भोंदू है? ....
9. आप ईमानदार क्यों नहीं हैं? ....
10. मैं चिड़चिड़ा नहीं हूँ। ....

Use of It

यह समय / दिन / महीना / साल इत्यादि बताने के लिए किया जाता है।
Time बताने के लिए to और past का प्रयोग करते हैं।
to का अर्थ होता है बजने में बाकी और past का अर्थ होता है बजकर।

Rule

It + is / was + minute + past / to + time

Ex.

1. सवा पाँच बज रहे हैं। — It is quarter past 5.
2. साढ़े पाँच बज रहे हैं। — It is half past 5.
3. पौने पाँच बज रहे हैं। — It is quarter to 5.
4. पाँच बज के दस मिनट हो रहे हैं। — It is 10 minutes past 5.
5. पाँच बजने में दस मिनट बाकी है। — It is 10 minutes to 5.

इसके अलावे 'it' के कई अलग तरह से प्रयोग किए जाते हैं।

Rule

It + is easy / difficult + unless / necessary to + V¹ + Object + O.W.

Ex:

1. अंग्रेजी बोलना आसान है। — It is easy to speak english.
2. अंग्रेजी बोलना कठिन है। — It is difficult to speak english.
3. हिन्दी बोलना बेकार है। — It is useless to speak hindi.
4. अंग्रेजी बोलना जरूरी है। — It is necessary to speak english.

Exercise

1. सवा नौ ....
2. साढ़े चार ....
3. पौने दस ....
4. 4 बजकर 10 मिनट ....
5. 6 बजने में 10 मिनट बाकी ....
6. फ्रेंच सीखना कठिन है। ....

7. धूप में दौड़ना बेकार है। ....
8. गाड़ी चलाना आसान है। ....
9. यहाँ आज जरूरी है। ....
10. अंग्रेजी अखबार पढ़ना आसान है। ....

	Subject	**Object**	**Possesive Case**
1.	I – मैं, मैंने	Me – मुझे, मुझको	My – मेरा, अपना
2.	You – आप, आपने	You – आपको, तुमको, तुम्हें	Your – तुम्हारा, अपना
3.	We – हम, हमने	Us – हमें, हमको	Our – हमारा, अपना
4.	He – वह, उसने	Him – उसे, उसको	His – उसका, अपना
5.	She – वह, उसने	Her – उसे, उसको	Her – उसका, अपना
6.	They – वे, उन्होंने	Them – उन्हें, उनको	Their – उनका, अपना

Use of was, were

Positive : Subject + was/were + other words.
Negative : Subject + was/were + not + other words.
Interrogative : Was/were + Subject + other words?
Negative : Was/were + Subject + not + other words?
Wh. : Wh. + was/were + Subject + other words?
Wh. Negative : Wh. + was/were + Subject + not + other words?

Was/Were

ID. – था, थे, थी, होता था, रहता था, होते थे, रहते थे।

He, She, It, Mohan, I → was

We, You, They, Boys → were

Ex.

1. तुम परेशान थे। You were upset.
2. तुम परेशान नहीं थे। You were not upset.
3. क्या तुम परेशान नहीं थे? Were you upset?
4. क्या तुम परेशान नहीं थे? were you not upset?
5. तुम परेशान क्यों थे? Why were you upset?
6. तुम परेशान क्यों नहीं थे? Why were you not upset?

Exercise

1. तुम चुगलखोर थे। ....
2. क्या तुम चापलूस थे? ....
3. क्या वह एक आलसी लड़की थी? ....
4. मैं शराबी नहीं था। ....
5. क्या तुम खुशमिजाज़ थे? ....
6. तुम्हारे पापा कल कहाँ थे? ....
7. वह एक भ्रष्ट नेता थे। ....
8. पुरानी फिल्म अश्लील नहीं होती थी। ....
9. ईमानदार लोग सुखी रहते थे। ....
10. क्या तुम कल घर पर थे? ....

Vocabullary

Back Biter	–	चुगलखोर	Sycophant	–	चापलूस	Lazy	–	सुस्त, आलसी
Boozer	–	शराबी	Jolly natured	–	खुशमिजाज	Corrupt	–	भ्रष्ट
Vulgar	–	अश्लील						

Use of has, have

Positive : Subject + has/have + other words.

Negative : Subject + has/have + not + other words.

Interrogative : Has/have + Subject + other words?

Negative : Has/have + Subject + not + other words?

Wh : Wh. + has/have + Subject + other words?

Wh. Negative : Wh. + has/have + Subject + not + other words?

Has/Have

ID. – रखना, के पास होना, अधिकार होना, संबंध होना

He, She, It, Mohan → has

I, We, You, They, Boys → have

Ex.

1. तुम्हारे पास एक किताब है। — You have a book.
2. तुम्हारे पास किताब नहीं है। — You have not a book./You don't have a book.
3. क्या तुम्हारे पास किताब है? — Have you a book?/Do you have a book?
4. क्या तुम्हारे पास किताब नहीं है? — Have you not a book?/Don't you have a book?
5. तुम्हारे पास किताब क्यों है? — Why have you a book?/ Why do you have a book?
6. तुम्हारे पास किताब क्यों नहीं है? — Why have you not a book?/ Why don't you have a book?

इसके अलावा आप इन सभी Tense को बनाने के लिए do/does + have का प्रयोग भी कर सकते हैं।

Exercise

1. मेरे पास 100 रुपए हैं। ....
2. नेहा के पास दौलत नहीं है। ....
3. उसे घमंड नहीं है। ....
4. क्या आपके पास इस काम के लिए समय नहीं है? ....
5. मुझे कोई समस्या नहीं है। ....
6. मेरे सर में दर्द है। ....
7. तुम्हारे पास मोबाइल क्यों नहीं है? ....
8. उसके पास कोई मौका नहीं है? ....
9. मेरे पास बाईक नहीं है? ....
10. उनके पास आई कार्ड है। ....
11. आपके पास ए.टी.एम. कार्ड क्यों नहीं है? ....
12. क्या आपके चार दोस्त हैं? ....
13. क्या उसके पास मेरा मोबाइल नम्बर नहीं है? ....
14. मेरे पास DSL का पता है। ....
15. क्या आपके पास 100 के छुट्टे/खुल्ले हैं? ....

Use of 'had'

Positive	:	Subject + had + other words
Negative	:	Subject + had + not + other words
Interrogative	:	Had + Subject + other words?
Negative	:	Had + Subject + not + other words?
Wh	:	Wh. + had + Subject + other words?
Wh. Negative	:	Wh. + had + Subject + not + other words?

Had

ID. – रखना, के पास होना, अधिकार होना, संबंध होना

He, She, It, Mohan → had

I, We, You, They, Boys → had

Ex.

1.	तुम्हारे पास एक किताब थी।	You had a book.
2.	तुम्हारे पास किताब नहीं थी।	You had not a book./You didn't have a book.
3.	क्या तुम्हारे पास किताब थी?	Had you a book?/Did you have a book?
4.	क्या तुम्हारे पास किताब नहीं थी?	Had you not a book?/Didn't you have a book?
5.	तुम्हारे पास किताब क्यों थी?	Why had you a book?/ Why did you have a book?
6.	तुम्हारे पास किताब क्यों नहीं थी?	Why had you not a book?/ Why did you not have a book?

इसके अलावा आप इन सभी Tense को बनाने के लिए did + have का प्रयोग भी कर सकते हैं।

Exercise

1. तुम्हारे पास मेरा मोबाइल था। ....
2. उसके पास अंतिम मौका था। ....
3. मेरे पास पैसा कमाने की तरकीब थी। ....
4. क्या आपके पास मेरे नोट्स थे? ....
5. मुझे कोई समस्या नहीं थी। ....
6. मेरे सर में दर्द था। ....
7. मुझे कोई उम्मीद नहीं थी। ....
8. उसकी एक अच्छी हैसियत थी। ....
9. मुझे मौत का डर था। ....
10. मुझे तुम्हारे प्रति सहानुभूति थी। ....
11. आपके पास मेरे नोट्स थे। ....
12. क्या आप के पेट में दर्द था? ....
13. क्या उसके पास मेरा पता नहीं था? ....
14. क्या आप के भाई के पास लैपटॉप था? ....
15. हमारे पास कोई मौका नहीं था। ....

Some Important Structure

Use of 'has to' and 'have to'

ID. – ना है, नी है, पड़ता है, पड़ती है।

Rules

1.	**Positive**	:	Subject + has to/have to + V^1 + Object + OW.
2.	**Negative**	:	Subject + has not to/have not to + V^1 + Object + OW.
3.	**Interrogative**	:	Has/have + Subject + to + V^1 + Object + OW?
4.	**Negative**	:	Has/have + Subject + not + to + V^1 + Object + OW?
5.	**Wh.**	:	Wh. + Has/have + Subject + to + V^1 + Object + OW?
6.	**Wh. Negative**	:	Wh. + Has/have + Subject + not + to + V^1 + Object + OW?

Ex.

1.	तुम्हें कल यहाँ आना है।	You have to come here tomorrorw.
2.	तुम्हें कल यहाँ नहीं आना है।	You have not to come here tomorrorw.
3.	क्या तुम्हें यहाँ कल आना है?	Have you to come here tomorrorw?
4.	क्या तुम्हें यहाँ कल नहीं आना है?	Have you not to come here tomorrorw?
5.	तुम्हें यहाँ कल क्यों आना है?	Why have you to come here tomorrorw?
6.	तुम्हें यहाँ कल क्यों नहीं आना है?	Why have you not to come here tomorrorw?

Use of 'was to' and 'were to'

ID. – ना था, नी थी

Rules

1.	**Positive**	:	Subject + was to/were to + V^1 + Object + OW
2.	**Negative**	:	Subject + was not to/were not to + V^1 + Object + OW
3.	**Interrogative**	:	Was /were + Subject + to + V^1 + Object + OW?
4.	**Negative**	:	Was/were + Subject + not + to + V^1 + Object + OW?
5.	**Wh**	:	Wh. + was /were + Subject + to + V^1 + Object + OW?
6.	**Wh. Negative**	:	Wh. + was /were + Subject + not+ to + V^1 + Object + OW?

Ex.

1.	तुम्हें कल यहाँ आना था।	You were to come here yesterday.
2.	तुम्हें कल यहाँ नहीं आना था।	You were not to come here yesterday.
3.	क्या तुम्हें यहाँ कल आना था?	Were you to come here yesterday?
4.	क्या तुम्हें यहाँ कल नहीं आना था?	Were you not to come here yesterday?
5.	तुम्हें यहाँ कल क्यों आना था?	Why were you to come here yesterday?
6.	तुम्हें यहाँ कल क्यों नहीं आना था?	Why were you not to come here yesterday?

Use of 'had to'

ID. – पड़ा था, पड़ी थी

Rules

1. **Positive** : Subject + had to + V^1 + Object + OW
2. **Negative** : Subject + had not to + V^1 + Object + OW
3. **Interrogative** : Had + Subject + to + V^1 + Object + OW?
4. **Negative** : Had + Subject + not + to + V^1 + Object + OW?
5. **Wh** : Wh. + had + Subject + to + V^1 + Object + OW?
6. **Wh. Negative** : Wh. + had + Subject + not + to + V^1 + Object + OW?

Ex.

1.	तुम्हें कल यहाँ आना पड़ा।	You had to come here yesterday.
2.	तुम्हें कल यहाँ नहीं आना पड़ा।	You had not to come here yesterday.
3.	क्या तुम्हें यहाँ कल आना पड़ा?	Had you to come here yesterday?
4.	क्या तुम्हें यहाँ कल नहीं आना पड़ा?	Had you not to come here yesterday?
5.	तुम्हें यहाँ कल क्यों आना पड़ा?	Why had you to come here yesterday?
6.	तुम्हें यहाँ कल क्यों नहीं आना पड़ा?	Why had you not to come here yesterday?

Use of 'will have to'

ID. – पड़ेगा, होगा

Rules

1. **Positive** : Subject + will have to + V^1 + Object + OW
2. **Negative** : Subject + will not have to + V^1 + Object + OW
3. **Interrogative** : Will + Subject + have to + V^1 + Object + OW?
4. **Negative** : Will + Subject + not + have to + V^1 + Object + OW?
5. **Wh** : Wh. + will + Subject + have to + V^1 + Object + OW?
6. **Wh. Negative** : Wh. + will + Subject + not + have to + V^1 + Object + OW?

Ex.

1. तुम्हें कल यहाँ आना पड़ेगा। — You will have to come here tomorrow.
2. तुम्हें कल यहाँ नहीं आना पड़ेगा। — You will not have to come here tomorrow.
3. क्या तुम्हें यहाँ कल आना पड़ेगा? — Will you have to come here tomorrow?
4. क्या तुम्हें यहाँ कल नहीं आना पड़ेगा? — Will you not have to come here tomorrow?
5. तुम्हें यहाँ कल क्यों आना पड़ेगा? — Why will you have to come here tomorrow?
6. तुम्हें यहाँ कल क्यों नहीं आना पड़ेगा? — Why will you not have to come here tomorrow?

Use of 'may have to'

ID. – पड़ सकता है।

Rules

Positive	:	Subject + may have to + V^1 + Object + OW.
Negative	:	Subject + may not have to + V^1 + Object + OW.
Interrogative	:	May + Subject + have to + V^1 + Object + OW?
Negative	:	May + Subject + not + have to + V^1 + Object + OW?
Wh	:	Wh. + may + Subject + have to + V^1 + Object + OW?
Wh. Negative	:	Wh. + may + Subject + not + have to + V^1 + Object + OW?

Ex.

1. तुम्हें कल सी.पी. जाना पड़ सकता है। — You may have to go to C.P. tomorrow.

Exercise

1. मुझे DSL में अंग्रेजी सीखनी पड़ सकती है। ....
2. क्या तुम्हें आज सी.पी. जाना पड़ सकता है? ....
3. क्या हमें यहाँ कल आना पड़ सकता है? ....
4. हमें यहाँ रोज आना पर पड़ सकता है। ....
5. मुझे तुम्हारी कार का ध्यान रखना पड़ सकता है। ....
6. पुलिस को यहाँ छानबीन क्यों करनी पड़ सकती है। ....
7. क्या तुम्हें पिछले महीने पटना जाना पड़ सकता है। ....
8. मुझे कल अपना मोबाइल बदलना पड़ सकता है। ....
9. क्या आपको मुझसे कल मिलना पड़ सकता है। ....
10. आपको आज क्या करना पड़ सकता है। ....
11. तुम्हें बाहर मेरा इंतजार करना पड़ सकता है। ....
12. मुझे अपने दोस्त को मनाना पड़ सकता है। ....
13. मुझे कल अपनी बाइक बदलनी पड़ सकती है। ....

USE OF 'ACQ AINTED WITH'

ID. – परिचित होना

Rules

1. **Positive** : Subject + h.v. (helping verb) + acquainted with + OW.
2. **Negative** : Subject + h.v. + not + acquainted with + OW.
3. **Interrogative** : H.v. + Subject + acquainted with + OW?
4. **Negative** : H.v. + Subject + not + acquainted with + OW?
5. **Wh** : Wh. + h.v. + Subject + acquainted with + OW?
6. **Wh. Negative** : Wh. + h.v. + Subject + not + acquainted with + OW?

Ex.

1. तुम राहुल गाँधी से परिचित हो। — You are acquainted with Rahul Gandhi.
2. तुम राहुल गाँधी से परिचित नहीं हो। — You are not acquainted with Rahul Gandhi.
3. क्या तुम राहुल गाँधी से परिचित हो? — Are you acquainted with Rahul Gandhi?
4. क्या तुम राहुल गाँधी से परिचित नहीं हो? — Are you not acquainted with Rahul Gandhi?
5. तुम राहुल गाँधी से परिचित क्यों हो? — Why are you acquainted with Rahul Gandhi ?
6. तुम राहुल गाँधी से परिचित क्यों नहीं हो? — Why are you not acquainted with Rahul Gandhi ?

Use of 'out of order'

ID. – खराब

Rules

1. **Positive** : Subject + h.v. (helping verb) + out of order.
2. **Negative** : Subject + h.v. + not + out of order
3. **Interrogative** : H.v. + Subject + out of order?
4. **Negative** : H.v. + Subject + not + out of order?
5. **Wh** : Wh. + h.v. + Subject + out of order?
6. **Wh. Negative** : Wh. + h.v. + Subject + not + out of order?

Ex.

1.	तुम्हारा मोबाइल खराब है।	Your mobile is out of order.
2.	तुम्हारा मोबाइल खराब नहीं है।	Your mobile is not out of order.
3.	क्या तुम्हारा मोबाइल खराब है?	Is your mobile out of order?
4.	क्या तुम्हारा मोबाइल खराब नहीं है?	Is your mobile not out of order?
5.	तुम्हारा मोबाइल क्यों खराब है?	Why is your mobile out of order?
6.	तुम्हारा मोबाइल क्यों खराब नहीं है?	Why is your mobile not out of order?

Use of 'get/don't get'

ID. – दे दीजिए, लाओ, मत होइए।

Rules

1. Get + Object + OW / Get + OW

2. Don't Get + OW

Ex.

1.	मुझे एक गिलास पानी दे दीजिए।	Get me one glass of water.
2.	मुझे अपना मोबाइल नम्बर दे दीजिए।	Get me your mobile number.
3.	एक खाली पेपर लाओ।	Get a blank paper.
4.	अपनी कार इधर लेके आओ	Get your car here.
5.	नर्वस मत होइए।	Don't get nervous.
6.	लेट मत होइए	Don't get late.

Use of 'Getting'

ID. – हो रहा है, हो रही है, हो रहे हो

Rules

1. Positive	:	Subject + h.v. (helping verb) + getting + OW.
2. Negative	:	Subject + h.v. + not + getting + OW.
3. Interrogative	:	h.v. + Subject + getting + OW?
4. Negative	:	h.v. + Subject + not + getting + OW?
5. Wh	:	Wh. + h.v. + Subject + getting + OW?
6. Wh. Negative	:	Wh. + h.v. + Subject + not + getting + OW?

Ex.

1. तुम घबरा रहे हो	You are getting nervous.
2. तुम नहीं घबरा रहे हो	You are not getting nervous.
3. क्या तुम घबरा रहे हो?	Are you getting nervous?
4. क्या तुम नहीं घबरा रहे हो?	Are you not getting nervous?
5. तुम क्यों घबरा रहे हो?	Why are you getting nervous?
1. तुम क्यों नहीं घबरा रहे हो?	Why are you not getting nervous?

Use of 'Not with standing'

ID. – ऐसा होते हुए भी

Rules

Not with standing + Sentence

1. ऐसा होते हुए भी आप उसकी मदद कर रहे हो।	Not with standing you are helping him.
2. ऐसा होते हुए भी आप सच नहीं बोल रहे हो।	Not with standing you are not speaking the truth.

Exercise

1. मैं आपके पापा से परिचित हूँ। ....
2. क्या आप DSL से परिचित हो? ....
3. क्या आप की कार खराब है? ....
4. मुझे एक कप चाय दे दीजिए। ....
5. उसे एक ग्लास दूध दे दीजिए। ....
6. बाजार से एक पेन लेकर आओ। ....
7. ऐसा होते हुए भी आप आराम नहीं कर रहे हैं। ....
8. ऐसा होते हुए भी आप उसे पढ़ा रहे हैं। ....
9. क्या आप बोर हो रहे हो? ....
10. मैं लेट नहीं हो रहा हूँ। ....

Use of 'make the most of'

ID. – पूरा-पूरा फायदा उठाना

Rules : **Make the most of + OW**

Ex.

1. अपने दोस्तों का पूरा-पूरा फायदा उठाओ। Make the most of your friends.
2. अपने प्रतिभा का पूरा-पूरा फायदा उठाओ। Make the most of your talent.

Use of 'an out and out'

ID. – पक्का

Rules : **Sub. + helping verb (h.v.) + OW**

Ex.

1. वह पक्का चुगलखोर है। He is an out and out back biter.
2. वह पक्का भोंदू है। He is an out and out lumpish.

Use of 'How about'

ID. – कैसा रहा

Rules : **How about + Other words.**

Ex.

1. आपका रिजल्ट कैसा रहा? How about your result.
2. आपका साक्षात्कार कैसा रहा? How about your interview.

Use of 'What about'

ID. – कैसा रहेगा

Rules **What about + V^4 + Other words.**

Ex.

1. आज मूवी देखना कैसा रहेगा। What about watching movie today.
2. आज अंग्रेजी बोलना कैसा रहेगा। What about speaking english today.

Use of 'What the use of'

ID. – क्या फायदा

Rules : **What's the use of + V^4 + other words**

Ex.

1. अब रोने से क्या फायदा What's the use of weeping now.
2. उसकी झूठी तारीफ करने से क्या फायदा What's the use of adulating him.

Use of 'V³ + is + V³'

1. टूट गया सो टूट गया — Broken is broken.
2. खो गया सो खो गया — Lost is lost.
3. बोल दिया सो बोल दिया — Spoken is spoken.

Exercise

1. अपने दोस्तों का पूरा-पूरा फायदा उठाओ। ....
2. अपने रिश्तेदारों का पूरा-पूरा फायदा उठाओ। ....
3. वह पक्का ढोंगी है। ....
4. वह पक्का धोखेबाज है। ....
5. आपका व्यवसाय कैसा रहा। ....
6. आपकी आज की कक्षा कैसी रही। ....
7. आज सी.पी. जाना कैसा रहेगा। ....
8. कक्षा में हिन्दी बोलने का क्या फायदा। ....
9. दूसरों पर हँसने से क्या फायदा। ....
10. अपना समय बर्बाद करने से क्या फायदा। ....
11. बोल दिया सो बोल दिया। ....
12. हो गया सो हो गया। ....

Causative Verbs

Use of Make

हँसना	Laugh	हँसाना	Make laugh
रोना	Weep	रूलाना	Make weep
भागना	Run	भगाना	Make run
देखना	See	दिखाना	Make see
समझना	Understand	समझाना	Make understand
खेलना	Play	खिलाना	Make play
पढ़ना	Read	पढ़वाना	Make read
खुश होना	Happy	खुश करना	Make happy
दु:खी होना	Sad	दु:खी करना	Make sad
सोना	Sleep	सुलाना	Make sleep
बैठना	Sit	बिठाना	Make sit
गाना	Sing	गवाना	Make sing
नाचना	Dance	नचाना	Make dance
बोलना	Speak	बुलवाना	Make speak

Rules : **Sub. + H.V. + make + Obj. + V¹.**

Ex.

1. तुम उसे हँसाते हो। — You make him laugh (present Ind.)
2. तुम उसे हँसा रहे हो। — You are making him laugh. (Present Cont.)
3. तुमने उसे हँसा दिया। — You made him laugh. (Past Ind.)
4. तुम उसे हँसा रहे थे। — You were making him laugh. (Past Cont.)
5. तुम उसे हँसा सकते हो। — You can make him laugh.
6. तुम्हें उसे हँसाना चाहिए। — You should make him laugh.

Exercise

1. वह मुझे दुखी करता है। ....
2. वह उसे खुश करता है। ....
3. क्या आप उससे किताब पढ़वा रहे हो? ....
4. मैं तुम्हें समझा रहा हूँ। ....
5. मेरी माँ मुझे प्रतिदिन सुलाती है। ....

6. तुम उसे आज अपने साथ क्रिकेट नहीं खेलाओगे ....
7. मैं तुम्हें समझा रहा हूँ। ....
8. मैं आज से उसे नहीं रूलाउँगा। ....
9. मैंने उससे अपने जूते पॉलिस करवाए। ....
10. मैं उसे नचवा रहा था। ....
11. क्या उसने तुम्हें क्लास में जमीन पर बिठाया था? ....

Use of 'get/have'

Rules : **Sub. + helping verb + get / have + obj. + V^3.**

Ex.

1. तुम अपनी शर्ट धुलवाते हो। You get your shirt washed.
2. तुम अपनी शर्ट धुलवाना चाहते हो। You want to get your shirt washed.
3. तुमने अपनी शर्ट धुलवा ली। You got your shirt washed.
4. तुम अपनी शर्ट धुलवाओगे You will get your shirt washed.
5. तुम्हें अपनी शर्ट धुलवानी है। You have to get your shirt washed.
6. तुम अपनी शर्ट धुलवा सकते हो। You can get your shirt washed.
7. तुम्हें अपनी शर्ट धुलवानी चाहिए। You should get your shirt washed.

Exercise

मैंने कल अपने बाल कटवा लिए। ....

उसने इस साल अपना घर बनवा लिया। ....

मुझे आज अपनी कार ठीक करवानी है। ....

क्या तुम उसे पिटवा सकते हो? ....

मैं अपनी शर्ट बदलवाना चाहता हूँ। ....

मैंने उससे गाना गवाया। ....

मैं उसे नहीं मरवा सकता। ....

तुम्हें अपना मोबाईल ठीक करवाना चाहिए। ....

मैं हर महीने अपनी बाईक रिपेयर करवाता हूँ। ....

मैं आज आप के लिए नोट्स टाइप करवाऊंगा। ....

Vocabullary

Tease	तंग करना;	Vex, heckle, harass
Incite	उकसाना	Instigate, provoke
Hamper	रूकावट डालना	Obstruct
Captive	लुभाना	Facinate
Banter	हँसी मजाक करना	Cut a joke

Use of 'Please have'

ID – कृपया लीजिए।

Rules : **Please have + other words**

Ex.

कृपया एक ग्लास पानी लीजिए। Please have a glass of water.

कृपया एक कप चाय लीजिए। Please have a cup of tea.

Use of 'Please do'

ID – जरा तो सही

Rules : **Please do + V^1**

Ex.

ज़रा बैठिए तो सही Please do sit.

जरा अंग्रेजी बोलिए तो सही Please do speak english.

Use of 'went off'

ID – हुआ, हुई

Rules : **Sub. went off + other words**

Ex.

मेरा इंटरव्यू बहुत अच्छा हुआ My interview went off very well.

Use of 'Bent on'

ID – तुला हुआ , तुली हुई।

Rules : **Sub. + is/am/are + bent on + V^4 + object**

Ex.

तुम अंग्रेजी सीखने पर तुले हुए हो। You are bent on learning english.

वह आपको बदनाम करने पर तुला हुआ है। He is bent on defaming you.

Use of 'has/have gone'

ID – हो गया है।

Rules : **Sub. + has/have gone + Other words**

Ex.

वह पागल हो गया है। He has gone mad.

वह अंधी हो गई है। She has gone blind.

Exercise

1. तुम मुझे परेशान करने पर क्यों तुले हुए हो? ....
2. तुम उसे मारने पर क्यों तुले हुए हो? ....
3. वह आवारा हो गया है। ....
4. तुम बदतमीज हो गया है। ....
5. जरा बोलो तो सही। ....
6. जरा बाहर जाओ तो सही। ....
7. मेरी SSC की परीक्षा बहुत अच्छी हुई है। ....
8. कृपया एक ग्लास दूध लीजिए। ....

Use of 'after all'

ID – आखिरकार

Rules : **After all + Tense**

Ex.

आखिरकार मैं आपका दोस्त हूँ। After all I am your friend.

आखिरकार वह मेरी बहन है। After all she is my sister.

Use of 'smart at'

ID – अच्छा होना, निपुण होना

Rules : **Sub. + h.v. + smart at + V^4 + Obj. + OW**

Ex.

आप अंग्रेजी बोलने में अच्छे हो। You are good at spcaking english.

मेरी माँ खाना बनाने में अच्छी है। My mother is good at cooking.

Use of 'sick of'/'fed up with'

ID – ऊब गया हूँ, तंग आ गया हूँ।

Rules : Sub. + h.v. + sick of/ fed up with + OW

Ex.

मैं जिंदगी से तंग आ गया हूँ। I am sick of/fed up with life.

Use of 'to be fond of'

ID – शौक है/था, शौकीन है/था।

Rules : Sub. + h.v. + fond of/ V^4 + Obj. + OW

Ex.

मैं अंग्रेजी बोलने का शौकीन हूँ। I am fond of speaking english.

उसे चाय पीने का शौक है। He was fond of taking tea.

Use of 'in the habbit of'

ID – की आदत है / थी

Rules : Sub. + h.v. + in the habit of + V^4 + Obj. + OW

Ex.

उसे अखबार पढ़ने की आदत है। He is in the habbit of reading newspaper.

उसे दिन में सोने की आदत थी। He was in the habbit of sleeping at noon.

Exercise

1. वह गणित से ऊब गई है। ....
2. मैं आपसे तंग आ गया हूँ। ....
3. मुझे मूवी देखने का शौक है। ....
4. उसे गाली देने की आदत है। ....
5. उसे गाना गाने का शौक नहीं था। ....
6. उसे किताब पढ़ने की आदत नहीं थी। ....
7. क्या तुम्हें शराब पीने की आदत है? ....
8. वह फ्रेंच बोलने में अच्छा है। ....
9. क्या आप कार चलाने में अच्छे हैं। ....
10. आखिरकार तुम मेरे पड़ोसी हो। ....

Use of 'remind'

ID – याद दिलाना

Rules : **Remind + Obj. + + V^1 + OW**

Ex.

मुझे बिजली का बिल जमा करने के लिए याद दिला देना	Remind me to pay the electricity bill.
उसे ऑफिस जाने के लिए याद दिला देना	Remind him to go to office.

Use of 'pose for'

ID – बना फिरता है।

Rules : **Sub. + pose for + OW**

Ex.

वह एक डॉक्टर बना फिरता है	He poses for a doctor.
आप नेता बने फिरते हो	You pose for a leader.

Use of 'will try'

ID – कोशिश करूँगा

Rules : **Sub. + will try to + V^1 + Obj. + OW**

Ex.

मैं उसे मनाने की कोशिश करूँगा	I will try to persuade him.
मैं आज से अंग्रेजी बोलने की कोशिश करूँगा।	I will try to speak english today onwards.

Use of 'to be about to'

ID – वाला है, वाली है, वाले हैं

Rules : **Sub. + h.v. + about to + V^1 + Obj. + OW**

Ex.

मैं आज फरीदाबाद जाने वाला हूँ।	I am about to go to Faridabad.
मेरा भाई आज यहाँ आने वाला है।	My brother is about to come here today.
मैं तुम्हें इस बारे में कल बताने वाला था।	I was about to tell you about it yesterday.

Use of 'just like that'

ID – यूँ ही, ऐसे ही।

Rules : **Tense + Just like that**

Ex.

मैं यहाँ यूं ही बैठा हुआ हूँ।	I am sitting here just like that.
वह बाहर ऐसे ही टहल रही है।	She is walking outside just like that.

Exercise

मुझे आज बाजार से सब्जी खरीदने के लिए याद दिला देना ....

उसे कोचिंग जाने के लिए याद दिला देना। ....

वह गलियों में हीरो बना फिरता है। ....

वह अपने आप में शिक्षिका बनी फिरती है। ....

मैं उसे बात-विवाद में हराने की कोशिश करूँगा। ....

तुम आज से अंग्रेजी समाचार पत्र पढ़ने की कोशिश करोगे। ....

क्या तुम्हारी मम्मी तुम्हें आज उपहार देने वाली है। ....

मैं कल आपके घर आने वाला था। ....

क्या आप अपने मित्रों के साथ मूवी देखने वाले हो? ....

मैं कल आपके घर आने वाला था। ....

तुम से यूँ ही बातें कर रहा हूँ। ....

वह ऐसे ही आपका प्रतीक्षा कर रही है। ....

Use of 'had better'

ID – अच्छा होगा या अच्छा हो

Rules : **Had better + Sub. + would + V^1 + Obj. + OW**

Ex.

अच्छा होगा तुम कक्षा में अंग्रेजी बोलो।	Had better you would speak english in the class room.
अच्छा होगा तुम बुरी संगति छोड़ दो।	Had better you would give up bad company.
अच्छा होगा वह इस साल एम.बी.ए. कर ले।	Had better he would complete M.B.A. this year.

Use of 'has/have/had been'

ID – रह चुका है/था, रह चुके हैं/थे।

Rules : **Subject + has/have/had been + OW**

Ex. लालू बिहार का मुख्यमंत्री रह चुके है।	Lalu has been the CM of Bihar.
कपिलदेव भारतीय टीम का कप्तान रह चुका है।	Kapil Dev has been the captain of Indian Team.
नेहरू जी देश के प्रधानमंत्री रह चुके थे।	Nehru had been the PM of India.

Use of 'ask'

ID – कहो

Rules : **Ask + obj. + to + V^1**

Ex. उसे बैठने के लिए कहो	Ask him to sit.
उसे पढ़ने के लिए कहो	Ask him to study.
उसे बाहर जाने के लिए मत कहो	Don't ask him to go outside.

Use of 'made for'

ID – बना हुआ होना

Rules : **Sub. + h.v. + made for + OW**

Ex. यह घर तुम्हारे लिए बना हुआ है।	This house is made for you.
यह लड़की तुम्हारे लिए नहीं बनी हुई है।	This girl is not made for you.

Use of 'used to/be/have'

ID – ता था, ती थी।

Rules : **Sub. + used to + V^1 + Obj. + OW**

There + used to be + OW

Sub. + used to have + OW

Ex.

मैं बचपन में मंदिर जाया करता था।	I used to go to temple in childhood.
हम बचपन में मूवी नहीं देखा करते थे।	We did not use to watch movie in childhood.
यहाँ एक स्कूल हुआ करता था।	There used to be a school here.
मेरे पहले लम्बे-लम्बे बाल हुआ करते थे।	I used to have long hair before.

Use of 'has ever/have ever'

ID – जितने/जितनी - उनमें सबसे।

Rules : **Sub. + h.v. + SD + Sub. + has/have ever + V^3**

Ex.

मैंने किताबें पढ़ी है। उनमें सबसे अच्छी किताब यह है।	This is the best book I have ever read.
मैंने जितनी मूवी देखी है उनमें सबसे अच्छी OMG है।	OMG is the best movie I have ever watched.

Use of 'would like to'

ID – चाहूँगा, चाहेंगे, चाहोगे

Rules : **Sub. + Would like to + V^1 + Object + OW**

Ex.

मैं यहाँ अंग्रेजी सीखना चाहूँगा	I would like to learn english here.
क्या आप मेरे साथ चाय पीना चाहोगे?	Would you like to have tea with me?
क्या आप आज आराम करना चाहोगे?	Would you like to take rest today?

Use of 'began to / started'

ID – लगा, लगी, लगे / शुरू कर दिया

Rules : **Sub. + began to + V^1 + Object + OW**

Sub. + started + V^4 + Object + OW

Ex.

वह हँसने लगी	She began to laugh.
तुमने अंग्रेजी बोलना शुरू कर दिया	You started speaking english.
क्या तुम कॉलेज जाने लगे?	Did you begin to go to college.

Use of 'came to know'

ID – पता चल गया

Rules : **Sub. + came to know + that + tense**

Ex.

उसे पता चल गया कि तुमने उसकी किताब चुराई थी।	He came to know that you stole his book.
मुझे पता चल गया कि तुम बेवकूफ हो।	I came to know that you are fool

Exercise

1. अच्छा होगा कि तुम अपनी गंदी आदतें सुधार लो ....
2. अच्छा होगा कि तुम अपनी पढ़ाई पर ध्यान दो। ....
3. अटल बिहारी भारत के प्रधानमंत्री रह चुके हैं। ....
4. राजीव गांधी देश के नेता रह चुके थे। ....
5. उसे अपना काम करने के लिए कहो। ....
6. उसे सोने के लिए मत कहो।। ....

7. यह कार उसके लिए नहीं बनी हुई है। ....

8. ये कुर्सियाँ आपके लिए बनी हुई है। ....

9. मेरे पास एक होंडा सिटी कार हुआ करती थी। ....

10. उसके पास एक स्कूटर हुआ करता था। ....

11. पहले यहाँ एक मंदिर हुआ करता था। ....

12. मैंने जितने भी कोचिंग देखे हैं उनमें सबसे अच्छा DSL है।

....

14. क्या आप मेरे साथ मूवी देखना चाहोगे? ....

15. क्या आप आज ऑफिस जाना चाहेंगे? ....

16. वह रोने लगी। ....

17. मैं ऑफिस जाने लगा। ....

18. उसने लिखना शुरू कर दिया। ....

19. मेरे पापा को पता चल गया कि मैं आवारा लड़का हूँ। ....

20. तुम्हारे मित्र को पता चल गया कि तुम उन्हें धोखा देते हो

....

21. शिक्षक को पता चल गया कि तुम कक्षा में दूसरों को परेशान करते हो।

....

Present Indefinite Tense

ID – ता है, ती है, ते हैं।

Rules : **Sub. + $V^{1/5}$ + Object + OW.**

Sub. + do/does + not + V^1 + Object + OW.

Do/does + Sub. + V^1 + Object + OW ?

Do/does + Sub. + not + V^1 + Object + OW ?

Wh. + do/does + Sub. + V^1 + Object + OW ?

Wh. + do/does + Sub. + not + V^1 + Object + OW ?

Ex.

1.	तुम मुझे जानते हो	You know me.
2.	तुम मुझे नहीं जानते हो।	You don't know me.
3.	क्या तुम मुझे जानते हो?	Do you know me?
4.	क्या तुम मुझे नहीं जानते हो?	Don't you know me?

5.	तुम मुझे क्यों जानते हो?	Why do you know me.
6.	तुम मुझे क्यों नहीं जानते हो?	Why don't you know me?
7.	तुम मुझे जानते हो न।	You know me don't you?
8.	तुम मुझे नहीं जानते हो न।	You don't know me do you?

- **To describe habitual or repeated action**
  Ex. – I teach you english here.
- **To describe movie**
  Ex. – Salman is an actor in Ek tha Tiger movie and he loves Katrina Kaif.
- **To describe recent past popular event.**
  Ex. – Baba Ramdev ends his fast at eleven O'clock.
  Vilash Rao passes away in the hospital.
- **To describe fixed future planning with time.**
  Ex. – Rahul Gandhi visits to UP tomorrow at seven a.m.

Some Important Structure

Use of 'keep'

ID – रहता है, रहते हो, रहती है।

Rules : **Sub. + keep/s + V^4 + Object + OW**
Sub. + do/does + not + keep + V^4 + Object + OW
Do/does + Sub. + keep + V^4 + Object + OW?
Do/does + Sub. + not + keep + V^4 + Object + OW?
WH. + do/does + Sub. + keep + V^4 + Object + OW?
WH. + do/does + Sub. + not + keep + V^4 + Object + OW?

Ex.

1.	तुम क्रिकेट खेलते रहते हो	You keep playing cricket.
2.	तुम क्रिकेट नहीं खेलते रहते हो	You don't keep playing cricket.
3.	क्या तुम क्रिकेट खेलते रहते हो?	Do You keep playing cricket?
4.	क्या तुम क्रिकेट नहीं खेलते रहते हो?	Don't You keep playing cricket?
5.	तुम क्रिकेट क्यों खेलते रहते हो?	Why do You keep playing cricket.
6.	तुम क्रिकेट क्यों नहीं खेलते रहते हो?	Why don't You keep playing cricket.
7.	तुम क्रिकेट खेलते रहते हो न?	You keep playing cricket don't you?
8.	तुम क्रिकेट नहीं खेलते रहते हो न?	You don't keep playing cricket do you?

Use of 'know how to'

ID – जानते हो, आती है, आता है, जानता है

Rules : Sub. + know how to + V^1 + Object + OW
Sub. + do/does + not + know how to + V^1 + Object + OW
Do/does + Sub. + know how to + V^1 + Object + OW ?
Do/does + Sub. + not + know how to + V^1 + Object + OW ?
WH. + do/does + Sub. + know how to + V^1 + Object + OW ?
WH. + do/does + Sub. + not + know how to + V^1 + Object + OW?

Ex.

1.	तुम क्रिकेट खेलना जानते हो	You know how to play cricket.
2.	तुम क्रिकेट खेलना नहीं जानते हो	You don't know how to play cricket.
3.	क्या तुम क्रिकेट खेलना जानते हो?	Do You know how to play cricket?
4.	क्या तुम क्रिकेट खेलना नहीं जानते हो?	Don't You know how to play cricket?
5.	तुम क्रिकेट खेलना क्यों जानते हो?	Why Do You know how to play cricket?
6.	तुम क्रिकेट खेलना क्यों नहीं जानते हो?	Why Don't You know how to play cricket?
7.	तुम क्रिकेट खेलना जानते हो न?	You know how to play cricket don't you?
8.	तुम क्रिकेट खेलना नहीं जानते हो न?	You don't know how to play cricket do you?

Exercise

1. तुम उसे परेशान करते रहते हो।
2. क्या आप दूसरों की चुगली करते रहते हो?
3. क्या आप को कम्प्यूटर चलाना आता है?
4. मुझे जर्मन बोलनी नहीं आती है।
5. आप अपने दोस्तो का मजाक क्यों बनाते हो?
6. आप उसे मेरे खिलाफ क्यों उकसाते हो?
7. तुम मेरे काम में बाधा क्यों डालते हो?
8. पुलिस रात में गश्त क्यों लगाती है?
9. तुम घर पर मेहनत क्यों नहीं करते हो?
10. वह तुम्हें बदनाम क्यों करती है?
11. तुम हमेशा मुझे धमकी क्यों देते हो?
12. तुम अपने दोस्तों की पढ़ाई में मदद क्यों नहीं करते हो?

Spoken Questions

1. Tell me about your daily routine.
2. Tell me about something you love/hate.
3. How do you spend your every sunday?
4. Which is your favourite city/colour/country/day of the week/ holiday/ festival/movie/ sports/T.V. Programme/ newspaper/mobile/temple/car/ place and why?
5. Who is your favourite actor/actress/cricket player/singer/teacher/leader/ friend and why?

Use of 'feel like to'

ID – मन कर रहा है या मन करता है।

Rules :

Sub. + feel like to + V^1 + Object + OW

Sub. + do/does + not + feel like to + V^1 + Object + OW

Do/does + Sub. + feel like to + V^1 + Object + OW ?

Do/does + Sub. + not + feel like to + V^1 + Object + OW ?

WH. + do/does + Sub. + feel like to + V^1 + Object + OW?

WH. + do/does + Sub. + not + feel like to + V^1 + Object + OW?

Ex.

1.	तुम्हारा मूवी देखने का मन कर रहा है।	You feel like to watch movie.
2.	तुम्हारा मूवी देखने का मन नहीं कर रहा है।	You don't feel like to watch movie.
3.	क्या तुम्हारा मूवी देखने का मन कर रहा है?	Do You feel like to watch movie?
4.	क्या तुम्हारा मूवी देखने का मन नहीं कर रहा है?	Don't You feel like to watch movie?
5.	तुम्हारा मूवी देखने का मन क्यों कर रहा है?	Why do You feel like to watch movie.
6.	तुम्हारा मूवी देखने का मन क्यों नहीं कर रहा है?	Why don't You feel like to watch movie.
7.	तुम्हारा मूवी देखने का मन कर रहा है न?	You feel like to watch movie don't you?
8.	तुम्हारा मूवी देखने का मन नहीं कर रहा है न?	You don't feel like to watch movie do you?

Use of 'want'

ID – चाहता हूँ, चाहता है, चाहती है, चाहते हैं।

Rules : **Sub. + want to + V^1 + Object + OW**
Sub. + do/does + not + want to + V^1 + Object + OW
Do/does + Sub. + want to + V^1 + Object + OW
Do/does + Sub. + not + want to + V^1 + Object + OW
WH. + do/does + Sub. + want to + V^1 + Object + OW
WH. + do/does + Sub. + not + want to + V^1 + Object + OW

Ex.

1. तुम अंग्रेजी सीखना चाहते हो। — You want to learn english.
2. तुम अंग्रेजी सीखना नहीं चाहते हो। — You don't want to learn english.
3. क्या तुम अंग्रेजी सीखना चाहते हो? — Do you want to learn english?
4. क्या तुम अंग्रेजी सीखना नहीं चाहते हो? — Don't You want to learn english?
5. तुम अंग्रेजी क्यों सीखना चाहते हो? — Why do you want to learn english?
6. तुम अंग्रेजी क्यों नहीं सीखना चाहते हो? — Why don't you want to learn english?

Use of 'like'

ID – पसंद करना।

Rules : **Sub. + like to + V^1 + Object + OW**
Sub. + do/does + not + like to + V^1 + Object + OW
Do/does + Sub. + like to + V^1 + Object + OW ?
Do/does + Sub. + not + like to + V^1 + Object + OW ?
WH. + do/does + Sub. + like to + V^1 + Object + OW ?
WH. + do/does + Sub. + not + like to + V^1 + Object + OW ?

Ex.

1. तुम किताबें पढ़ना पसंद करते हो। — You like to read books.
2. तुम किताबें पढ़ना पसंद नहीं करते हो। — You don't like to read books.
3. क्या तुम किताबें पढ़ना पसंद करते हो? — Do You like to read books ?
4. क्या तुम किताबें पढ़ना पसंद नहीं करते हो? — Do you not like to read books ?
5. तुम किताबें पढ़ना क्यों पसंद करते हो? — Why do you like to read books ?
6. तुम किताबें पढ़ना क्यों पसंद नहीं करते हो? — Why do you not like to read books ?
7. तुम किताबें पढ़ना पसंद करते हो न? — You like to read books don't you?
8. तुम किताबें पढ़ना पसंद नहीं करते हो न? — You do not like to read books, do you?

Use of 'it takes'

ID – लगता है, लगती है, लगते हैं

Rules : **It takes + Object + time to + V^1 + OW**
It + does not + take + Object + time to + V^1 + OW
Does + It take + + Object + time to + V^1 + OW ?
Doesn't + It take + Object + time to + V^1 + OW ?
WH. + does + it take + Object + time to + V^1 + OW ?
WH. + doesn't + it take + Object + time to + V^1 + OW ?

Ex.

1.	तुम्हें यहाँ आने में एक घंटा लगता है।	It takes you one hour to come here.
2.	तुम्हें यहाँ आने में एक घंटा नहीं लगता है।	It doesn't take you one hour to come here.
3.	क्या तुम्हें यहाँ आने में एक घंटा लगता है?	Does It take you one hour to come here.
4.	क्या तुम्हें यहाँ आने में एक घंटा नहीं लगता है?	Doesn't It take you one hour to come here.
5.	तुम्हें यहाँ आने में एक घंटा क्यों लगता है?	Why does it take you one hour to come here.
6.	तुम्हें यहाँ आने में एक घंटा क्यों नहीं लगता है?	Why doesn't it take you one hour to come here.

Exercise

1. मेरा आज किताब पढ़ने का मन नहीं कर रहा है। ....
2. क्या आप का सोने का मन कर रहा है। ....
3. क्या आप मुझे बदनाम करना चाहते हो? ....
4. मैं तुम्हें धमकी नहीं देना चाहता हूँ ....
5. क्या तुम दूसरों की चुगली करना पसंद करते हो? ....
6. तुम दोस्त बनाना पसंद क्यों नहीं करते हो? ....
7. मुझे यहाँ आने में दस मिनट लगते हैं। ....
8. तुम्हें चाय बनाने में कितना समय लगता है? ....
9. तुम्हें घर पहुँचने में कितना समय लगता है? ....
10. मेरा बकवास करने का मन नहीं कर रहा है। ....
11. तुम मेरी तलाशी क्यों लेना चाहते हो? ....

Spoken Questions

1. How do you spend your free time?
2. What kind of people do you like and dislike?
3. What are your goals in your life and how would you achieve them?
4. Do children learn bad habbits at school or at home?
5. Do you think it is better to be single or to be married?
6. Some people say that "books are best friends" is that true for you?
7. Do you give money to beggars or home less people? Why or why not?
8. Do you like to watch movie with your friends or your family? Why or why not?

Use of Past Indefinite

ID – या, ई, या था।

Points :

Last Year – पिछले साल

Last Month – पिछले महीने

Last Week – पिछले सप्ताह

Last Sunday– पिछले रविवार

Last night – कल रात   Yeaserday – कल

Day before yesterday – परसों

Any accident/incident – कोई दुर्घटना/घटना

Any last events like marriage/birthday party – कोई पार्टी / समारोह

School days – स्कूल के दिन   Childhood days – बचपन के दिन

2001 – 02, 02, 04

Rules :

Sub. + V^2 + Object + OW

Sub. + didn't + V^1 + Object + OW

Did + Sub. + V^1 + Object + OW ?

Didn't + Sub. + V^1 + Object + OW ?

WH. + did + Sub. + V^1 + Object + OW ?

WH. + didn't + Sub. + V^1 + Object + OW ?

Ex.

1. तुमने कल उसे परेशान किया था। — You vexed him yesterday.
2. तुमने कल उसे परेशान नहीं किया था। — You didn't vex him yesterday.
3. क्या तुमने कल उसे परेशान किया था? — Did you vex him yesterday ?
4. क्या तुमने कल उसे परेशान नहीं किया था? — Didn't you vex him yesterday ?
5. तुमने कल उसे परेशान क्यों किया था? — Why did you vex him yesterday ?
6. तुमने कल उसे परेशान क्यों नहीं किया था? — Why didn't you vex him yesterday ?
7. तुमने कल उसे परेशान किया था न? — You vex him yesterday didn't you ?
8. तुमने कल उसे परेशान नहीं किया था न? — You didn't vex him yesterday did you ?

Some Important Structure

Use of 'Kept'

ID – रहता था, रहते थे, ता रहा, ती रही।

Rules : Sub. + kept + V^4 + Object + OW
Sub. + did + not + keep + V^4 + Object + OW
Did + Sub. + keep + V^4 + Object + OW ?
Did + Sub. + not + keep + V^4 + Object + OW ?
Wh. + did + Sub. + keep + V^4 + Object + OW ?
Wh. + did + Sub. + not + keep + V^4 + Object + OW?

Ex.

1. आप कल मूवी देखते रहे। — You kept watching movie yesterday.
2. क्या आप कल मूवी देखते रहे? — Did you keep watching movie yesterday ?
3. आप कल मूवी क्यों देखते रहे? — Why did you keep watching movie yesterday.

Use of 'wanted'

ID – चाहता था, चाहती थी, चाहते थे।

Rules : Sub. + wanted to + V^1 + Object + OW
Sub. + did + not + want to + V^1 + Object + OW
Did + Sub. + want to + V^1 + Object + OW ?
Did + Sub. + not + want to + V^1 + Object + OW ?
Wh. + did + Sub. + want to + V^1 + Object + OW ?
Wh. + did + Sub. + not + want to + V^1 + Object + OW ?

Ex.

1. तुम उसे मारना चाहते थे। You wanted to kill him.
2. तुम उसे नहीं मारना चाहते थे। You didn't want to kill him.
3. क्या तुम उसे मारना चाहते थे? Did you want to kill him.
4. क्या तुम उसे नहीं मारना चाहते थे? Didn't you want to kill him.
5. तुम उसे क्यों मारना चाहते थे? Why did you want to kill him.
6. तुम उसे क्यों नहीं मारना चाहते थे। Why didn't you want to kill him.

Use of 'felt like to'

ID – मन करता था, मन कर रहा था

Rules : Sub. + felt like to + V^1 + Object + OW
Sub. + did + not + feel like to + V^1 + Object + OW
Did + Sub. + feel like to + V^1 + Object + OW ?
Did + Sub. + not + feel like to + V^1 + Object + OW ?
Wh. + did + Sub. + feel like to + V^1 + Object + OW ?
Wh. + did + Sub. + not + feel like to + V^1 + Object + OW ?

Ex.

1. तुम्हारा मूवी देखने का मन कर रहा था। You felt like to watch movie.
2. तुम्हारा मूवी देखने का मन नहीं कर रहा था। You didn't feel like to watch movie.
3. क्या तुम्हारा मूवी देखने का मन कर रहा था? Did you feel like to watch movie?
4. क्या तुम्हारा मूवी देखने का मन नहीं कर रहा था? Didn't you feel like to watch movie?
5. तुम्हारा मूवी देखने का मन क्यों कर रहा था? Why did you feel like to watch movie?
6. तुम्हारा मूवी देखने का मन क्यों नहीं कर रहा था? Why didn't you feel like to watch movie?

Exercise

1. तुम उसे पढ़ाते रहते थे। ....
2. मैं हर साल अपनी कार बदलता रहता था। ....
3. क्या तुम उसके बारे में सोचते रहते थे? ....
4. तुम्हारा कल अंग्रेजी बोलने का मन क्यों नहीं कर रहा था? ....
5. मेरे पापा मुझे वकील बनाना चाहते थे। ....

6. मैं पिछले साल एमबीए करना चाहता था। ....
7. क्या तुम कल बैंक से पैसे निकालना चाहते थे। ....
8. मैंने उसके साथ छेड़छाड़ नहीं की। ....
9. क्या पुलिस ने उसे नंगे हाथों पकड़ लिया था? ....
10. मैं अपनी ग्रेजुएशन 2006 में कर चुका हूँ। ....
11. तुमने उसे गाली क्यों दी थी? ....
12. क्या तुम्हारा लिखने का मन नहीं कर रहा था? ....

Use of Future Indefinite

ID – या, ई, या था।

Rules : **Sub. + will + V^1 + Object + OW (Other word)**
Sub. + will + not + V^1 + Object + OW
Will + Sub. + V^1 + Object + OW ?
Will + Sub. + not + V^1 + Object + OW ?
Wh. + will + Sub. + V^1 + Object + OW ?
Wh. + will + Sub. + not + V^1 + Object + OW ?

Ex.

1. तुम उसकी मदद करोगे। You will help him.
2. तुम उसकी मदद नहीं करोगे। You won't help him.
3. क्या तुम उसकी मदद करोगे? Will you help him?
4. क्या तुम उसकी मदद नहीं करोगे? Will you not help him?
5. तुम उसकी मदद क्यों करोगे? Why will you help him?
6. तुम उसकी मदद क्यों नहीं करोगे? Why won't you help him?
7. तुम उसकी मदद करोगे न? You will help him, won't you?
8. तुम उसकी मदद नहीं करोगे न? You won't help him, will you?

To Express Conditional Sentence

1. यदि तुम मुझे खून दोगे तो मैं तुम्हें आजादी दूँगा If you give me blood, I will give you freedom
2. अगर वह मुझसे मिलेगा तो मैं उससे बात करूँगा If he meets me, I will talk to him.
3. अगर आज वर्ज़ा होगी तो मैं ऑफिस नहीं जाऊँगा If it rains today, I won't go to office.
4. जब तक वह नहीं आएगा मैं उसका यहाँ इंतजार करूँगा I will wait for him untill he comes.

5.	अगर तुम मेहनत नहीं करोगे तो मैं तुम्हें नहीं पढ़ाऊँगा	If you don't work hard, I won't teach you.
6.	जब तक तुम मुझसे बात नहीं करोगे मैं यहाँ से नहीं जाऊँगा	I won't go from here unless you speak to me.

Who express opinions / speculations about future

We used many verbs, for example –

I think he will come

I hope he will go.

I expect you will speak english. (उम्मीद करना)

I suppose/assume you will do hard work. (मानना)

I believe god will help me.

I am sure she will come back.

I feel the weather will change.

I am afraid it will rain. (डर लगता है)

I wonder he will speak french. (विश्वास नहीं होता है)

I know you will help him.

Going to future

Talking about a decision or a plan made before the time of speaking.

❑❑❑

Unit-2

Greeting People
(लोगों का अभिवादन करना)

When people meet and greet each other they exchange certain words or expressions. In English language, there are several words and expressions people use between them on meeting or leaving each other, going on a journey and so on. Greetings are not the same. A friendly greeting is different from greeting a stranger. The present unit deals with the language people use on meeting or parting from each other at different parts of the day.

Informal Greetings (शुभकामना/बधाई/अभिवादन)

Greeting friends and familiar people
'**Hello!**' to your friends or someone you are close to when greeting them for the first time or at any time in the course of a day.

Remember (याद रखना)

"**Hello!**' is the most common friendly way of greeting people. The reply tc **Hello** is **Hello**. In American English people say, '**Hi**' instead of '**Hello**' wher greeting each other.

- **Good morning!** (प्रातःकालीन अभिवादन, शुभ प्रभात)
  '**Good morning**' when greeting someone in the morning.
  Remember : the time between the sunrise and the middle of the day is called morning.
- **Good after noon!** (दोपहर कालीन अभिवादन/नमस्कार)
  'Good afternoon' when greeting someone in the afternoon.
  Remember : afternoon begins at lunchtime and ends between five or six p.m.
- **Good evening!** (सायं कालीन अभिवादन/ शुभ संध्या)
  'Good evening' when greeting someone in the evening.
  Remember : evening is the period between the end of the afternoon and the time when you go to bed.
- **Good night!** (रात्रिकालीन अभिवादन/ शुभ रात्रि)
  Night' is the **period of time** between the sunset and midnight. It also means '**dark hours**' when most people are asleep.

- **Good day : (old-fashioned)**

Used when greeting or leaving someone during the day, but no longer used now.

- **How are you? (आप कैसे हैं?)**

How are you?' is an informal greeting used when a person inquires about someone's health and welfare.

Look at the examples:

- Hello! How are you? / How are you, Monika?
- Hi, how are you doing? (Am Eng)

Possible answers (संभावित उत्तर)

(a) Fine, thanks. How are you?
(b) Very well, thanks.
(c) OK, thanks.
(d) Fine, thank you. And you?

- **If someone is unwell, say: (अगर कोई अस्वस्थ है तो, कहें)**

How are you feeling now?
Are you all right? / Are you OK?
Reply: I'm feeling much better now.

- **Asking about other members of a family: (परिवार के अन्य सदस्यों के बारे में पूछने के लिए)**

How's your father? /How's your mother?
Reply : He's alright/She's fine, too.

- **If not well, say : (अगर स्वस्थ नहीं हैं तो कहें)**

He's not feeling well/She's down with fever.
She's (= she has) caught a cold.
He's (= he has) got chicken pox, etc.

How do you do? (Formal greeting)
आप कैसे हैं? (औपचारिक अभिवादन)

Note: "How do you do?" and "How are you" are not the same. and "How are you" are not the same. "How are you?" is an **informal** greeting used to inquire about someone's health and welfare.
"How do you do?" is a **formal** greeting (in question form) used when a person **introduces** himself to someone for **the first time**.

Look at the examples: Deepak: I'm Deepak from Delhi. Mr Yogi: How do you do?

Look at the example :

Deepa : I'm Deepa from Delhi.

Raj : How do you do? (Shaking hands)
Please to meet you.

Deepa : How do you do?

- **When leaving people, say: (लोगों से विदा लेते समय, कहिये)**

Goodbye! (More formal than 'bye' or 'bye-bye')

"Goodbye" is also used at the end of :

A telephone conversation, a radio or TV broadcast.

Look at the examples (इन उदाहरणों को देखें)

(a) Well, I've got to go now. Goodbye! See you tomorrow. (See = meet)
Response : Goodbye!

(b) Goodbye and thank you for a lovely dinner!
Response : Not at all !

(c) A tearful Goodbye at the airport
Vinod : I'll miss you very much !
Kajal : Me too, Goodbye !

- **Bye/bye-bye**

Most commonly used expressions between friends and relatives.

Look at the examples (इन उदाहरणों को देखें)

- I'm off now. See you next week, bye ! (Off = going)
- I'll give you a ring tomorrow, bye-bye.

Below are some more informal ways of parting:

नीचे विदाई के कुछ और अनौपचारिक तरीके दिये गये हैं :

OK. See you, then, bye ! /See you later, bye !
See you again_bye-bye ! See you at 8.30 bye !

These expressions can also be used when parting from someone:

Have a good time! /Have a good day! /Have a nice day!

But : When leaving somebody for an evening

Say : Have a nice evening! (Have- fun)

Your answer could be : Thank you. I will.

Cheerio (शुभ विदाई, नमस्कार) : (British slang) (अंग्रेजों की बोलचाल की भाषा में)

This is most informally used when leaving someone, eg:

(i) Kishan : OK, I'll ring you tomorrow morning, cheerio !
Preeti : Bye, have a nice day !

(ii) I'm late. I must fly now (= go fast).
Cheerio then! See you tomorrow !

Take care! (अपना ख्याल रखना) (= Take care of yourself)

Used when saying goodbye to family or friends, eg.
Bye, take care! See you next week.

- **Going on holiday(s) (छुट्टी/अवकाश पर जाते समय)**

When somebody is going on a holiday (= vacation)
Say : Have a good holiday! (Or) Have a good time!
On returning home : Welcome back/welcome home.

❑❑❑

Unit-3

Introducing Yourself and Others

(अपना और दूसरों का परिचय कराना)

In everyday life you often meet people who are strangers to you. You want to know them and have friendship with them, but you hesitate, feel nervous! What makes you so? obviously, the problem is your language. The purpose of this unit is to teach you the basics of introduction so that you could get over your shyness, interact with people confidently and have friendship with them.

Introducing yourself (अपने बारे में बताना)

(a) When meeting someone for the first time
Say : Hello! (Shaking hands) I'm Amit. (Give your name/surname)

(b) My name's Sumit. (My name is...)
(Or) I'm called Sumit. What's your name?

- **It is wrong to say :** Myself Amit
  The correct is : I'm Sumit/I'm Bhatia, (or) I'm Sumit Bhatia.
  Remember : "Myself" is the object pronoun and as such cannot be used in place of subject in the sentence.

- **If you want to introduce someone else**
  (अगर आप किसी और का परिचय करना चाहते हैं)

  Say : I'd like you to meet Mr Verma, (I'd=I would)
  (or) Here's Mr Verma, a friend of mine from Delhi.

- **Don't say.** He is/she is..., etc. (When introducing someone)
  Say : This is/that is

  Look at the examples :

  This is Kanika. (**Not :** She's Kanika). **That's** Tom. (**Not :** He's Tom)
  (or) : **Here's** Kanika. **She's** a student. **There's** Tom **He's** my brother.

Names and titles (नाम और उपाधियाँ)

First name/middle name/surname

The name of a person usually consists of three parts: first name, middle name and the last name. The **last name** of a person is his **surname** or the **family name** that he shares with all the members of his family, e.g : **Gupta**, **Sharma**, **Chatterji**, etc. The name that comes before the middle name is called **first name**; the name between the first name and the surname is called **middle name**.

Look at the example:
Surendra **(first name)**; Kumar **(middle name)**: Jha **(surname)**

Titles (उपाधियाँ)

Titles such as: Mr, Miss, Ms, Mrs are formally used with full names or surnames. But, they are usually avoided with names of people you know well or who are famous. As for the title **Ms** (pronounced as '**Miss**'), most women like it to use before their name these days because they don't wish to be identified as married.

Note : in written English, '**full stop**' at the end of a title (eg. Mr.) is not used; the shortened spelling is now generally accepted, eg. **Ms** Monika (Not Ms. Kanika)

Take care not to say or write 'Mrs and Mr': the correct is : Mr and Mrs, e.g. **Mr** and **Mrs** Kapadia are coming to dinner this evening.

■ How do you do? (आप कैसे हैं?)

This is a polite and more formal way of greeting strangers than friendly **"Hello".**

After greeting a stranger with "How do you do?" words of welcome are often used.

Look at the following examples:

- Glad to meet you / Nice to meet you / Pleased to meet you.
- Nice meeting you (especially in the U.S)

Use these expressions in your everyday speech:

How nice of you to come!

(**Say :** when thanking someone for coming)

Nice to see (not meet) you.

(**Say :** on meeting someone you already know)

It has/it's been nice **meeting** you.

(**Say :** when leaving someone you have just met.)

Formal introduction: introducing yourself and others

(औपचारिक परिचय : अपना और दूसरों का)

Look at the examples:

(a) **Moni** : Gunjan, this is Amit. He's from Delhi.

Gunja : Hello, how do you do? (Shaking hands)

Amit : How do you do? Are you from Mumbai?

Gunja : No, I'm from Goa.

(b) **Sonal** : This is Mr Sharma.

Gunja : How do you do? Pleased to meet you. Mr Sharma : How do you do?

(c) **Amit : That's Peter, a friend of mine from Delhi.**

He's a senior sales executive in our company.

Mr Sinha : Oh, nice to meet you! (Am Eng)

(d) **At the air port (हवाई अड्डे पर)**

Mr Raj : My name's Abhijeet Raj.

I'm from the United States.

Mr Sinha : Glad to meet you/Nice to meet you.

❑❑❑

Unit-4 Countries, Naionalities and Languages

(देश, राष्ट्रीयता और भाषाएँ)

■ Asking people where they are from

(लोगों से पूछना कि वे कहाँ से हैं?)

After a formal introduction you would like to know where people are from, what city or country they belong to, what languages they speak and a lot more about their personal life. This unit deals with all these in the following paragraphs.

Consider the following phrase (निम्न मुहावरों पर विचार करें)

Come from (जन्म लेना/पैदा होना) : used to inquire about the place or country a person belongs to.

Here are some examples (यहाँ कुछ उदाहरण दिये गये हैं)

Q. Where do you **come from** (originally)?

Ans. I come from a small village in Punjab.

Q. Where do the Gurkha soldiers **come from**?

Ans. They come from Nepal.

Q. Where does Bob **come from**?

Ans. He comes from London.

■ Where are you from? (What country/place...?)

आप कहाँ से हैं? (किस देश/ स्थान .....?)

Look at the examples :

Q. Where are you from?

Ans. I'm from a village near Delhi.

Q. Where are these tourists from?

Ans. They're from Spain.

Q. Hey, where are you from?

Ans. Mumbai? Me too!

Q. Where's Sonal from?

Ans. She's from Bangalore.

Q. Where's Bob from?

Ans. He's from London.

- **Native (मूल निवासी/देशवासी) : someone born in a particular country or region, eg.**
  - Tom was born in England. He is a **native** of England.
  - Catherine was born in France. She is a **native** of France.
  - Mr Kaushik was born in Delhi. He's a **native** of Delhi.

  Look at the examples:
  - Tom is **English**. (= He's a native of England)
  - He **comes from** England. (= He's from England)
  - Catherine is **French**. (= She's a native of France)
  - She **comes from** France. (= She's from France)
  - Mr Kaushik is **Indian**. (= He's a native of India)
  - He **comes from** India. (= He's from India)

- **Where do you live (now)? आप कहाँ रहते हैं (वर्तमान में)?**

  I live in Delhi. (= My home is in Delhi)

  Q. Where does your friend live?

  Ans. He lives in Agra.

  Q. Where does John live?

  Ans. He lives in England.

  Q. Where do these boys live?

  Ans. They live in Manipur.

- **What's your home address? (आपके घर का पता क्या है?)**

  I live at 94/3 Goss Burton Road.

  Since when have you **been/lived in** Delhi?

  (or) Since when have **you been living in** Delhi?

  I've been/lived in Delhi since 1975.

  (or) **I've been living in** Delhi **since** 1975

  Note : 'Since' is used with perfect tenses. It indicates a definite point of time in the past until now.

Conversations (वार्तालाप)

(a) **Mr Joshi** : Where do you live, Mr Verma?

Mr Verma : I live in Canada.

Mr Joshi : Are you Canadian?

Mr Verma : Yes, I am. (Not: I'm)

Mr Joshi : What's your address in Canada?
Mr Verma : I live at 159 Queens Road in Waterloc.

(b) **Kanika** : Do you live in Mumbai?
Rekha : No, I don't. I'm from Katmandu.
Kanika : What place do you live in there?
Rekha : I live in the suburbs (= away from the city).
Kanika : How long have you been here? (= Staying here)
Rekha : l've been here for two weeks.
Kanika : What nationality are you?
Rekha : I'm Nepalese
Kanika : What's your address in Nepal?
Rekha : I live at 35/61 in Golepara Colony.

Live/living (जीना/निवास करना/रहना)

Live (v) : expresses stability, permanent, eg.
I live in Agra. = My home is in Agra)

Living : suggests a short period of time, eg.
I'm living and working in Delhi these days.
Mr Barua's living in Mumbai just now.
He lives in Assam (= His home is in Assari)

- **Stay (at/in) (ठहरना, रहना) : expresses time spent temporarily in a place, e.g.**
  - When he goes to Mumbai he prefers to stay at in some hotel?
  - Why don't you stay in the youth hostel?
  - We stayed in London for three months.

- **People speak different languages (लोग विविध भाषाएँ बोलते हैं)**

Learn the following words and phrases:

- **A little (थोड़ा सा) :** not much, eg. She speaks a little English.
  Mr John can speak **a little** Hindi.
- **Well (अच्छा) :** satisfactorily, eg. He speaks English well/very well.
- **Pretty well (बहुत बढ़िया) :** quite well, eg. Amit speaks English pretty well.
- **Fluently (बेधड़क, धरक्के से, धाराप्रवाह) :** able to speak very well.
  He speaks English fluently. (= with ease and confidence)
  Shc's from south, but speaks Hindi **fluently**.

- **Perfectly** (पूरी तरह से, संपूर्णत:) **:** faultlessly, eg.
  He lived in France. He can speak French **perfectly**.
- **Exceptionally well** (असाधारण रूप से अच्छा) **:** unusually well, eg.
  He speaks English exceptionally well.
- **Broken English** (टूटा-फूटा) **:** English with lots of mistakes, eg.
  He explained how the accident took place in broken English.

Conversations (वार्तालाप)

Vinod : What's John's native language?
Kunal : He speaks English.
'English' is his native language.
It's his **mother tongue** (= the first language)
Vinod : What about his accent?
Kunal : His accent is rather Scottish. (= a bit)
He speaks English fluently.
Vinod : And Ms Catherine? Can she speak English?
Kunal : **A little**. She can speak a little English.
Vinod : What about her friend from the US?
Can she speak English?
Kunal : Yes. She speaks English **perfectly**.
Vinod : How **good** is her **accent** in English?
Kunal : She has a perfect American **accent**.
Vinod : What about Catherine's pronunciation?
Kunal : She has a lot of trouble **with** her pronunciation.
She talks in **broken English** with a **French** accent.
Vinod : Can you speak English, Sonal?
Anita : Yes, a little but I'm bad at pronunciation.
Vinod : How well does your sister speak English?
Anita : She speaks English pretty well.
Her **accent** is very good.
But at times she **makes** mistakes in grammar.
Vinod : Do you understand John's English?
Anita : Yes, I do. I understand him **perfectly**.
He's **fluent** in English.
Vinod : What do you think of the BBC newsreaders?
Anita : Their English is **exceptionally** (= extremely) well. ❑❑❑

Unit-5 Asking About Age

(उम्र के बारे में पूछना)

- When you ask someone: **"How old are you?"** The usual answer is: **I'm twenty years old**, etc; but this is a **formal** way of speaking about one's age.

  Remember : in spoken English, number **(+ years old)** is not used together.

  Don't say : I'm twenty years old.

  Say : I'm twenty. (Avoid 'years old')

  Look at the examples :

  How old are you? **I'm twenty**. How old is your father? He's fifty.

  How old is Gita? **I think** she's **about 25**.

  Note the following adverbs:

- **Nearly** (लगभग, करीब-करीब) (almost), e.g. :

  Q. : How old is your father?

  Ans : He's **nearly** sixty.

- **Quite** (बिल्कुल/पूर्ण रूप से) (completely), e.g. :

  Q. : How old is your brother?

  Ans : He isn't **quite** eighteenth.

  Q. : How old is your sister?

  Ans : She's **quite** young.

- **Yet** (अभी तक) (up to now), e.g. :

  Can you guess how old is my mother?

  Is she fifty five? No, but that's very **close**.

  Actually, she isn't fifty five **yet**.

  She'll be fifty five **next Friday**.

- **Still** (अब तक) (even to this time), e.g. :

  Q. : How old is your brother?

  Ans : He's **still** in his **twenties**.

  (**Twenties** = between 20 and 30)

  Say : in thirties/forties/fifties, etc.

Look at the examples :

He's in his **early thirties** (= below thirty five)

In late thirties = above thirty five.

Couple of = some/a few

Say : He's a couple of years/months... etc, older than me.

Don't say : He's older **than** I am. (Formal)

Say : He's older **than me**. (Spoken form)

Don't say : You are as young **as** she is. (Formal)

Say : You are as young **as her**. (Spoken form)

Note : object pronouns are used when as and than function as prepositions. If they function as conjunctions, they are followed by a clause.

- **We don't usually say :** "What's your age?" (Formal)

  Say : "How old are you?" (Spoken form)

Look at these examples:

Q. : What age are you? (= What's your age?)
Ans : I'm thirty.
Q. : What age is your father? (= What's your father's age?).
Ans : He's sixty.
Q. : What ages are your children, Smith?
Ans : Their ages are 9, 13 and 21(= they're 9, 13 and 21)
I have three children: 9, 13 and 21 years of age.

- **Look at the following expressions:**

The same age/your age/of your age

Examples :

- Kavita is/kavita's **the same age** as me.
- When I was **your age** I worked very hard.
- I have a son **of your age**.
- She has married a divorcee who's **twice her age**.

- **Consider these expressions:** (इन अभिव्यक्तियों पर विचार करें :)

At what age? /at the age of/at an early age/at my age, etc.

Here are some examples :

At what age do children go to school in your country?

- He died **at the age of** 80/She died **at an early age** (= very young)
- I passed my first degree exam **at your age**.

- I was a boy **at his age**, etc.

Age (v) : He's/he is **ageing** fast (= growing old fast)

■ If a person turns.... (He becomes that age)

Say : How old is your father?

He's/he has just **turned** 50. (= He has reached/passed that age.)

Look at these examples :

Q. : How old are you?

Ans : I've just **turned** thirty.

Q. : How old is your sister?

Ans : She **turned** twenty six on 14th last month.

He still looks quite young although he's (= he has) **turned** forty.

■ On the wrong side of more than (Used formally)

Examples :

Q. : How old is Babita's mother?

Ans : She's **on the wrong side of** 50. (= She's older than 50)

Q. : How old is her husband?

Ans : Appears to be **on the wrong side** of 55.

■ Elder/eldest (बड़े/सबसे बड़े)

Look at the example :

Wrong : He is elder than me.

Right : He is **older** than me.

Elder of the two :

(a) Who is **elder** (= older) of you?

I am his **elder** (= older) brother.

(b) My **elder** sister is at university (= older than me)

She is **three** years older than me.

■ Consider the following (निम्न पर विचार करें :)

Mr Dass has three children: two sons and one daughter.

Their ages are: 15, 10 and 7.

Abhinav is 15, Monu is 10 and Golu is 7. Abhinav is **older than** Monu.

Monu is five years **younger than** Abhnav.

Who's (= who is) **older of** the two?

Who's the **oldest/youngest** of the three?

Monu will say :

Abhinav is my elder brother. He's **older than** me.
He's five years **older than** me. I'm **older than** Golu.

Golu will say :

Monu is my **elder** brother. He's **older than** me.
Abhinav and Monu are **older than** me.
They're my **elder** brothers. Abhinav is **the eldest** in the family.

Golu will say : He's my eldest brother.

Monu and Golu will say : Abhinav is **the eldest** of us three.

Mr Dass will say:

Abhinav is my **eldest** son. (= He's the first born)
He's **the oldest** of the three.

- **Below are given some phrases:**

A **10-year** old boy/**40-year** old man, A **60-year** old woman, etc.

Look at the examples:

Operate (on/upon): = perform surgery
A team of surgeons operated upon a 10-year old boy.
A **60-year** old woman was operated on for a tumour.
A **40-year** old man was arrested for cheating.

❑❑❑

Unit-6 Asking About Occupation

(पेशा/व्यवसाय के बारे में पूछना)

- **Asking and answering questions** (प्रश्न पूछना और उत्तर देना)

Say : What do you do? (= what's your job?)

Remember : when you say : "What do you do?" you mean the same as "What's your job?" or "What's you profession?"

Look at the examples :

Q. : What do you do?
Ans : I'm a doctor. I work in a hospital.
Q. : What does your father do?
Ans : He runs a small business.
Q. : What does your mother do?
Ans : She's a housewife.

Here are some more examples :

Q. : What do you do, Priya ?
Ans : I'm a student.
Q. : What does your brother do?
Ans : He's at college. (= Studying)
Q. : Is your father a doctor?
Ans : No, He's bank manager.
Q. : What do you do?
Ans : I haven't got a job. (= I'm unemployed)

- **There is another way of asking about one's job**
(यहाँ नौकरी के बारे में पूछने का एक और तरीका दिया गया है)

Q. : What are you? (= What do you do?)
Ans : I'm a student.
Q. What's your father" (= What does your father do?)
Ans : He's a doctor.
Q. : What's Mrs Verma?
Ans : She's a homemaker.
Q. : What's her husband?
Ans : He's an architect.

Q. : What business are you in?
(Mention the particular business you deal in)

Ans : I'm in shoe business. (= I trade in shoes)
I deal in ready-made garments/electronics goods.
Or firm/company deals in refrigerators, etc.Z

- **Questions and answers (प्रश्न और उत्तर)**

Q. : What work do you do?
Ans : I do repair work.
Q. : What work does she do?
Ans : She's Yoga teacher.
Q. : What work does Ravi do?
Ans : He's a publisher.
Q. : What's your work?
Ans : My work is farming. (= I do farming)
Q. : What's his work?
Ans : His work is typing. (= He's a typist)

Learn how to use the following phrases
(निम्न मुहावरों का प्रयोग करना सीखें)

Set up; take up

Set up (स्थापित करना, बुनियाद रखना) = establish; start one's own business, e.g.

- He plans to **set up** his own business.
- He has **set up** as an interior designer.
- (or) he has set **himself** as an interior designer.

Take up (विचार करना) : start a job, e.g.

- He's (= he has) resigned to take up a more lucrative job.

Lucrative (लाभदायक व्यवसाय) : a business or job that earns you a lot of money.

He took up photography as his living/she took up teaching post.

Learn the uses of : at, in , for, as

'At' refers to the **place** where someone goes regularly to work.

'In' suggests **inside/within** a place of work.

Work for = do a job (for)

Look at the following sentences :

- He works **for** the BBC but I don't know what his job is.

- She teaches science **at** an intermediate college.
- He's an electrical engineer **in** a big company.
- He's a lecturer **at/in** a college/university.
- She works **for** a computer company.
- He teaches **in** a school/college.
- He works as a manager **in** a bank.
- She works **at** the local hospital.

▪ There are three categories of workers :

(श्रमिकों की तीन श्रेणियां हैं :)

(a) Skilled workers (कुशल श्रमिक)

Some jobs require **highly trained** and **experienced** workers. Carpenters, weavers, etc. are called **skilled** workers.

(b) Unskilled workers (अकुशल श्रमिक)

Workers who need **strength** rather than **skill**, e.g. Labourers/porters, etc; they are untrained : (Without any special training)

(c) Semi-skilled workers (अर्द्ध कुशल श्रमिक)

They are **untrained** still need some **skill** to do their job.

▪ Learn the following as well :

At work (= working)

Shift (पारी/पाली) : a period when workers in a factory, hospital, etc. are at work.

Look at the examples :

- Don't disturb the labourers; they'are at work. (= working)
- Are you on the night **shift** or the day **shift**?

Below are some more words and expressions :

- **Apply for a job (नौकरी के लिए आवेदन करना)**

  He's (= he has) applied **for** a job **at** the university.

- **On the job (कार्यरत) :** working/busy

  Please tell me how many workers are **on the job**.

- **Leave a job (नौकरी छोड़ना) :** give up one's job

  He's (= he has) decided **to leave** his job.

- **Look for a job (नौकरी की तलाश में) :** try to find a job

  I'm looking for a new job.

- **Out of a job (नौकरी से बाहर) :** unemployed; jobless
  He's (= he has) been **out of** a job for months.
- **Take a job (नौकरी पाना) :** accept the job, e.g. :
  I've **taken the job** of a clerk.
- **Loose one's job (नौकरी खोना) :** no longer has it.
  He's (= he has) **lost** his **job**.

■ **Lay-off** - हटा देना
If someone is **laid off**, he has been told by his employer **to leave** the job, e.g. :
In private industries sudden **lay-off** are very common/they've **laid off** 50 workers.
The company has decided to **lay** us **off** for two months/he's been **laid off** for a month.
What would you do if you get **laid off**? Would you start looking for another job?

■ **Parity (समानता) :** equality; being at par, e.g.
They're on strike for **parity** of pay/we want **pay parity** with fellow workers.

■ **Perk (भत्ता)** (usually plural) : advantages that you get in addition to your pay, e.g.
There are nice **perks** with the jobs provided by multinational companies.
He'll have a furnished house, a car and a cell-phone as **perks** with the job.

■ **Increment (इजाफा/बढ़ोतरी) :** the amount you get with your salary every year, e.g.
The starting salary is Rs. 8000/- p.m.
In addition, you'll have an annual increment of rupees 100/-

■ **What is your job like? (आपका काम कैसा है?)**
What's your job like (= Describe the job you are doing)
Say : It's a good/very interesting/boring/tiring job.
It's a hard work/hazardous occupation. (= Risky/dangerous)

❑❑❑

nit-7

The Place You Live in

(स्थान जहाँ आप रहते हैं)

House (घर)

house' is a building for people to live in. **'Home'** is the permanent address ere you live with your family; it may be a flat, an apartment, a mansion or y other building. 'Home' is more than

'Home' also indicates a person's **place of birth**. When you say, **"I'm going home"** You are referring to a country or the place you were born in.

Look at these examples :

- After finishing his studies he left America for **'home'**.
- After getting married to an NRI she now looks on London as her **'home'**.

Don't say : I'm going to my house/ Go to your house you're tired.
Say : I'm going **home**/Go home you're tired.
Note : When speaking of movement towards home, 'to' is not used.

Here are some more examples :

- He went **home**/she came **home**/we arrived **home** late.
- Did he get **home** early?/they're leaving **home** tonight.

Also : drove **home**/brought **home,** etc.

At home (Br Eng.)

'At home' means in or at the place where you live, e.g. :
I'm **at** home means, "he is in the house".
But : in American English home is used without 'to', e.g. :
Let's stay **home** this evening/Is your mother **home**?
'At' is optional. Look at these examples :
Where's he? (= Where is he?)
He is/he's **(at) home**. Is she **home**? Yes, she's **home** now.
Were you **home**? Where's he gone? (= Where has ....?)
He has/he's gone **home**.
He has/he's **been home** twice this month. (= Visited home)
Consider these as well :

He stays **(at)** home/lives **(at)** home/works **(at)** home.

She keeps a servant **(at)** home.

Short forms :

Kanika + is = Kanika's

At Madhu's (+ noun) = at Madhu's home.

Say : The Guptas (= Mr and Mrs Gupta and family)

Types of Buildings (भवनों के प्रकार)

People live in different **types** of houses : some are **large** and **expensi** and only the rich can afford to live. But, most people live in buildings th have several **floors**.

Floor (मंजिल) : a level of a building; storey.

- There can be several floors **in** a building, e.g.
- Ground floor/first floor/second floor/third floor ....../top floor.

Look at the examples :

- Our office is **on** the ground floor/she has a two-bed roomed grou floor flat.
- He lives **on** the first floor/there's a coffee bar **on** the top floor/plea take these suitcases **to** the second floor/I'm going **to** the tenth flo etc.

■ **Lift :** a machining or an apparatus **in a tall** building that people **ride** to move **up** and **down** between the floors. This is called **elevator** in t US.

Look at the examples :

- Please, **take** the lift **to** the top floor/they **took** the lift down **to** t ground floor.
- I don't like going **in** a lift/what if we got stuck **in** a lift!

■ **Storey (मंजिल) :** a floor is called **storey** in British English, e.g.

- A single **story** building is quite safe/she lives in a three-storey hou
- I saw a **multi-story** car park/their new house has **five storeys,** e

Say : she works in a **five-storey/storeyed** building.

New York is a city of multi-storey/storeyed building.

■ **Flat/Apartment (मकान/अपार्टमेंट)**

A flat in British English means a number of rooms to live in on one floo a larger building.

My sister lives in a **flat**/He lives in an **apartment** in New York, etc.

There can be several rooms and locations in a home, e.g.

Sitting room; living room; drawing room; study; bed room; bathroom; toilet; dining room; kitchen; pantry; store; staircase; lobby; landing; porch; terrace; shed; basement; patio, garage, etc.

A brief description of each location is given below :
(प्रत्येक स्थान का संक्षिप्त विवरण नीचे दिया गया है :)

A sitting room/living room in a house or an apartment is the main room where people sit and relax together but don't usually eat there; a **drawing room** (formally called) is used to receive guests; a **study** is a room for reading, writing and studying.

A **pantry/larder** is a small room used for storing food; an **attic** is a room at the top of a house; a **staircase** in a building is a set of stairs usually with a rail that you can hold on as a support.

A **landing** is a flat area at the top of a staircase; a **terrace** is a flat roof used to enjoy the fresh air.

The following words are used in everyday speech :

Upstairs (ऊपर की मंजिल) : the upper floor(s) of a building.

Downstairs (नीचे की मंजिल) : the ground floor (down a staircase).

In everyday speech people generally say
(रोजमर्रा के बोलचाल में लोग आमतौर पर कहते हैं :)

"What's your house like?" (= What kind of house do you have)
Say this when requesting someone to describe his or her house.

Conversation (वार्तालाप)

Amit : What's your new house like, Anita?
Anita : It's very nice, most modern and big enough.
It has/ it's got two bedrooms, a sitting room, a kitchen, and a bathroom.
Amit : Don't you have a basement?
Anita : No. But we've got a large backyard.
Amit : Where do you sleep, upstairs?
Anita : No, I don't but my parents sleep. They live upstairs.
My brother, sister and I sleep downstairs.
Amit : Hey! You've got a very big house.

❑❑❑

Unit-8 Addressing Word
(संबोधन शब्द)

Informal address (औपचारिक संबोधन)

(a) addressing parents and close relatives
(माता-पिता और करीबी रिश्तेदारों को संबोधित करना)

The following words can be used to address parents :

- **Mother :** Mum/Mom/Mommy/Mummy/Mama/ Ma.
- **Father :** Pa/Papa/Dad/Daddy

Note: 'father' and 'mother' are rather formal in British English.

Words such as :

Aunt/auntie/uncle is informally used in every day speech,

e.g. Hello, aunt/auntie! Shila! How are you?
Sit down, uncle. Can I speak to Uncle Ram, please?

Note : Aunt is more formal than auntie.

(b) Words expressing love and affection
(प्यार और स्नेह को प्रकट करने वाले शब्द)

- **Sweetie :** someone you are fond of, younger children,
  e.g. : Oh, my sweetie! /Hello, sweetie! /Just a minute, sweetie!
- **Baby :** a very young child, who is unable to speak or walk
  e.g. : Don't rush up the stairs, baby.
  Oh, come on, baby/I love you, baby/don't touch it, baby!
- **Love :** People use this word to address their loved ones.
  Look at the example: Don't cry, my love!
  What has/what's happened to you, my love?
- **Dear** (प्रिय, प्यारा) **:** a word of affection, e.g.
  How are you, dear? /Can I use your pencil, dear?
  Tell me dear, "Where have you been all this time?"
- **Sweetheart** (प्रिय, प्रियतम) **:** used to address a person you love ve[ry] much.
  A couple uses it to each other; a child is addressed as sweetheart,
  e.g. Don't cry my sweetheart!
  Have this toffee, sweetheart, etc.

- **Darling** (प्रिय, प्यारा) **:** used to address someone you love, e.g. : a member of your family.

  Ex : Here's your coffee darling, why all this hurry?

  What can I get you darling, etc.?

- **Honey** (colloquial) : used to someone you love, (Am. Eng)

  Ex : (A mother to her children)

  Which frock would you like, my honey?

  Sit down here, my honeys.

  (Between a pair of lovers to each other)

  Hi, honey! Why the rush? Where are you going?

  Happy birthday, my honey!

Friendly forms of address (मित्रवत संबोधन के तरीके)

- **Man :** used esp. when you are excited/annoyed/angry/impatient, etc.

  For example : Stop talking nonsense, man! /Hurry up, man!

  Don't shout, man!

- **Buddy :** (slang) a close friend of a man, e.g.. We're good buddies.

  Hey, buddy! (in anger): get out of this room, buddy!

  Gulshan and I have been great buddies for years.

- **Chap :** used to address a man or boy, e.g.

  Come on, you chap. Let's go for a picnic.

  You old chap, where were you?

  Sit down, you chaps.

- **Guy :** used to address a man or boy, eg.

  Hello, guy! How are you? / Please drive slowly, guy.

  Mrs. Gupta (to her husband): Guy, have you paid the bill?

- **Guys :** (in plural) can be used to address a group of:

  (a) People (male or female)

  (b) Men.

Look at the examples:

- Hey, you guys! Don't shout here/Come on, you guys.
- Hey, you guys! Where are you going?!

Note : 'hey' is used to call attention or to express surprise.

- **How to address people who are known to you:**

Use the first name to address a person you know well.

Look at the example :

Naresh, can you tell me what film is on at the Plaza?
If relations are formal, use **Mr/Miss, etc. + surname**, e.g.
Mr Gupta, can you lend me some money?
Put your signature here please, Miss Sonam.

- **Formal address (औपचारिक संबोधन)**

Say : "Excuse me!" to attract the attention of a stranger, e.g.
Excuse me, can you tell me the way to the station, please?
Excuse me, Madam! Is there a post office near here?
Excuse me! Are you Mr Sinha?

- **Ladies and gentlemen!**

Say this if you are addressing:

(a) A formal opening of a speech
(b) A meeting/crowd/conference, etc.

Look at the examples :

Ladies and gentlemen! It's my privilege and pleasure to ...

- **Sir :** used to address a man to whom you wish to show respect. This can also be used to address an older man or a man in authority. Soldiers and policemen address their officers as **"Sir"**. School children address Male teachers as **"Sir"** at school. (**Opp :** Miss)

Note : a female teacher is addressed as **Miss** whether married or unmarried.

A shop assistant addresses his male customer as "Sir" in a shop or restaurant.

- **Madam/Ma'am** (= Spoken form)
- **Madam :** a polite and respectful way of addressing a woman whether married or unmarried. In places like a shop or restaurant women customers are addressed as madam/ma'am.
- **Madam**. Women holding **official positions** are also addressed as **Madam**.

  Say : Madam Prime Minister/Madam President
  Madam Chairperson. (Also: 'chairwoman')

  (Opp) : Mr President/Mr Prime Minister, etc.

Occupation as a form of address (संबोधन के रूप में व्यवसाय)

Look at the examples :

- **Doctor**
  Good morning, doctor! /May I have a word with you, doctor?
  Thank you, doctor, etc.

- **Nurse :**
  Nurse, I'm cold. Give me a blanket, please. (Don't say: feeling cold)
  Please call the doctor, Nurse.
  Note : 'feel' is normally not used in the continuous form except in a medical sense, e.g.
  I'm not feeling well/she's feeling giddy, etc.

- **Officer :**
  This is used for persons in authority, e.g.

There are some special forms of address (संबोधन के विशिष्ट तरीके)

- **Your Majesty!** (महाराज)
  A title is used to address a king or queen, e.g.
  - **Your Majesty,** the Prime Minister's here to see you.
    People are against the new bill, Your Majesty.
    Thank you, **Your Majesty**.
    Note : bill is a proposal for a new law.

- **Your Highness!** (महाराजा / महारानी)
  A title is used to address a member of the royal family (prince/princess, etc), e.g
  - **Your Highness**, the Queen Mother wants to see you.
  - Thank you, **Your Highness**!
    Note : Queen Mother is the mother of a ruling king or queen.

- **My Lord!** (मेरे स्वामी/मालिक/प्रभु) (British English) :
  This is used to address very high-ranking people and other officials, e.g.
  - Would you sign the paper, My Lord/I beg your pardon, **My Lord!**
  - There are some people waiting for an audience (meeting) with you, **My Lord**/Excuse me, **My Lord!** You're wanted on the phone

- **Your Lordship! His Lordship!**
  This is a respectful way of addressing **judges, bishops**, etc.
  - If **your lordship** gives me time, I can produce the evidence.

- I feel honoured to meet you, **your lordship**.

- **Your Excellency!** (महामहिम)

  This title is used to address very **high-ranking** officials, e.g. Ambassadors, High commissioners, Governors, etc. e.g.
  - You're welcome to The City of Taj, **Your Excellency**.
  - **Your Excellency**, the delegation is waiting for you.

- **Your Honour** (जज साहब)

  This is used when speaking to a **judge**:
  - Does this case require any more evidence, **Your Honour**?
  - That's all, **Your Honour!** This is all what I wanted to say in this case.
  - **Your Honour** the accused is innocent of the crime, etc.

- **Honourable!** (माननीय)

  This is used to address high officials, eg: MPs, Ministers, etc.

  Here are some examples:
  - Will the Honourable Member please, sit down?
  - Honourable Minister Mr. Desai is not present in the house, sir.
  - The **Honourable justice** has not pronounced the decision yet.

❑❑❑

Unit-9

Polite behaviour/Nature
(विनम्र व्यवहार/स्वभाव)

- **Please and thank you (कृपया और धन्यवाद)**

'Please' and 'thank you' are expressions of courtesy. Please' is often used when you make polite enquiries, requests or want to attract someone's attention.

- **Thank you/thanks (धन्यवाद)**

These are expressions of appreciation for someone's favour or kindness. Thanks' is commonly used when people are with friends and family. **"Thank you"** is rather **formal** and is often used to **accept things**.

- **Thank you very much (बहुत-बहुत धन्यवाद)**

Sometimes stronger expressions are needed than the plain 'thank You', for example,

Say : "Thank you very much" if you want to express your feelings of happiness and satisfaction in a stronger way.

Say : :Thanks a lot" or "Many thanks" when someone gives you a present or does something special for you.

- **Responses to 'thank you' or 'thanks'**
('धन्यवाद' या 'धन्यवाद' के जवाब)

(a) **That's all right/It's all right** (formal)
Used as a polite reply when someone has thanked you

(b) **It's OK /That's OK** (informal):
Commonly used to say : 'there is no need to thank me.'

(c) **It's my pleasure!**
Used when you want to say: ;I was pleased to help, you.'

(d) **You're welcome** (Am Eng):
Say this to someone who has just thanked you.

(e) No problem (Am Eng): used to say, 'It doesn't matter.'

(f) Not at all/don't mention it:
Used to say : 'there is no need to thank me'

- **Here are some more examples:**

(a) Oh, how kind of you! Thank you very much.

Response : No problem

(b) **Sumit :** Could you post these letters, please?
Moni : With pleasure
Sumit : Thanks a lot!
Moni : That's all right

(c) Thank you very much.
I couldn't have done it without your help!
Response : Oh, it's my pleasure.

(d) Thank you for coming to see us!
Response : It's all right.

(e) **Kishan :** Can you lend me some money?
Vinod : Sure! Kishan: Thanks a lot! Vinod : Not at all

(f) Please give me your pen.
Thanks!
Response : It's OK.

(g) When does the Taj Express leave Agra for Delhi?
At seven in the evening
Thank you.
Response : you're welcome/it's a pleasure.

(h) Thank you for a lovely dinner!
Response : Not at all ! We enjoyed having you.

(i) Here's your birthday present, Mohini.
Oh, that's lovely ! Thank you very much.
Response: It's OK.

(j) Many thanks for your support!
I don't know I'd have done without you. (I'd = I would)
Response : Don't mention it. I'm pleased to help you.

(k) Thank you for a wonderful party, Sonia.
Response : Not at all! We've enjoyed, too.

(l) Can you get me to the airport by 7.30?
Response : By all means
Thank you.
Response : My pleasure

(m) **At the interview:**
Chairman: Well, I wish you the best of luck and thank you for joining us.
Candidate: Thank you.

❑❑❑

Unit-10 Making Requests
(अनुरोध करना)

- **Making requests (अनुरोध करने के लिए)**

The commonest way of making a request is to use the expression :

"Will you?"

In modern English this is much more used than any other form of request.

Here are some examples :

- **Will you** open the window? (= Please open the window)
- **Will you** shut the door? (= Please shut the door)

A request can be made more polite by adding "Please"

Look at the examples :

- **Will you** open the window, **please** ?
- **Will you please** pass me the butter?

Responses : Yes, of course.

(or) I'm sorry I can't.

- **Would you?**

"Would you?" is more polite than "will you?"

It expresses the speaker's hesitation.

The use of "kindly" makes the request all the more polite.

Look at the examples :

- Will you hold the door open for me?
- **Would** you hold the door open for me?
- Will you kindly post this letter for me?
- **Would** you **kindly** post this letter for me?
- Will you kindly stop smoking here?
- **Would** you **kindly** stop smoking here?
- Will you please give him this letter?
- **Would** you **please** give him this letter?

- **The following expression are questions :**

(1) Do you mind? (= Would you object to ....?)

(2) Would you mind?(= Would you object to ....?)

Look at the exmaples :

- Do you **mind** if I smoke?/Do you mind my **smoking**?
- Would you **mind** if I smoke?/Would you mind my **smoking**?
- Would you mind shutting the door?
(= Please shut the door)
- Would you **mind** not **shutting** the door?
(= Please don't shut the door)
- Excuse me! Would you **mind** not **smoking** here?
(= Please don't smoke here)
- Would you **mind turning** your TV down a little?
(= Please reduce the loudness ......)

▪ **Consider the following examples :**

Q. : Do you mind if I borrow your pen?
Ans : yes, by all means
Q. : Do you mind if I use your telephone?
Ans : Of course you can ! (or) I'm sorry (you can't).
Q. : Do you mind my smoking here?
Ans : Not at all
I'd rather you didn't. (= Please don't smoke here)

Look at the examples :

Q. : Do you mind if I smoke?
Ans : Yes, I do mind. I hate smoking. (emphatic)
Q. : Would you mind if I use your towel?
Ans : sorry!
Q. : Would you mind if I turn off the TV?
Ans : Oh, sure (= No, I wouldn't)

▪ **When offering something to someone**

(किसी को कुछ भेंट करते समय)

Say : Will you ....?

Examples :

- Will you have some tea?/Won't you have some tea?

Q. : What will you have, tea or coffee?
Ans : I'll have some coffee, please. (or) No, thank you.

Take care not to say : No, I won't.

- **"Would" makes the offer more polite**
(Would प्रस्ताव को और अधिक विनम्र बनाता है।

Q. : Would you have tea? What would you prefer?
Ans : I'd prefer some tea and roasted potatoes. (I'd = I would)
Q. : What would you **rather** have? (Rather = prefer to)
Ans : Wouldn't you have some coffee? No, thank you.

- **Would you like? (क्या आप चाहेंगे?)** (= Do you want?)

The above expression is commonly used to make a polite request or an offer.

Note : the phrase I'd like (= I want) is used to answer a request.

Consider the following examples :

Q. : What would you like to have?
Ans : I'd like to have some tea, please.
Q. : Would you like some coffee?/Wouldn't you like some coffee?
Q. : Would you like another cup of coffee?
Ans : No, thank you. One cup is enough.
Q. : What would you like for breakfast?
Ans : I'd like some sandwiches, please.
Q. : What would you like to have, a cold drink or hot drink?
Q. : Would you like anything else?
Ans : No, thank, you.
Q. : Would you like to go to the movie this evening?
Ans : Yes, I would. Thank you.
(or) No, I'd **rather** stay home. I'm tired. (Rather = perfer to .....)

Conversation (वार्तालाप)

Soni : I'd like fifty rupees, Mum.
Mum : What for?
Soni : I'd like some pencils, a sketch pen and a notebook.
Dad : How many pencils would you like?
Soni : I'd like two pencils and a rubber for school work.

Reena wants some books.
She'd like a magazine, too. (= she wants .....)

A little more polite way of introducing a request

Note the following expressions :

Could I?/Could you?/couldn't you?

Look at the examples :

Q. : Excuse me, **could you** tell me the time, please?
Q. : Could I possibly leave the office an hour earlier today?
Ans : No, not today please.
Q. : Could I have a glass of water, please?
Ans : Sure.
Q. : Could you tell me the way to the airport?
Ans : You mean the new one?
Q. : Could I have your name, please?
Ans : Yes, I'm called Mohit Khanna.
Q. : Could I use your pen?
Ans : By all means.
Q. : Could you post these letters, please?
Ans : With pleasure!
Q. : Could you please mend my radio?
Ans : Certainly.
Q. : **Couldn't you** come a little earlier?
Ans : Well, I'll try my best.

Unit-11 Asking for Permission

(इजाजत के लिए पूछना)

- The following words are commonly used to express the idea of permission :
  Can/Could/May/Might
  Can I ......?
  Remember : the use of 'Can I ?' is the commonest and most informal way of requesting for permission. People use it frequently with friends and family.

Asking for permission (अनुमति/इजाजत के लिए पूछना)

Questions	**Answer**
Can You do me a favour?	Sure
Can I speak to your father?	Sorry, not just now.
Can I speak to your mother, then?	Yes, of course you can
Can I use your telephone?	Yes, of course.
Mum, can I go out and play?	No, you can't

(On the phone)

Q. : Hello, can I speak to Soni, please?
Ans : Please, hold on.

- **Could I .....?** (A polite alternative to 'can')
  Remember :
  'Could' is more 'hesitant' and polite than 'can.'

Look at the examples :

Questions	**Answer**
Could I ask you a question?	Oh, sure.
Could I use your telephone?	Yes, of course you can
Could I speak to the principal, please?	Sorry, he's busy at the moment.
Could I have a word with your father?	I'm afraid you can't (= I'm sorry)

Note : though 'could' is past in form, it has nothing to do with the past time here.

- **May I ......?**
  Note : the use of 'May' is more formal, polite and respectful.

Look at the examples :

Questions	**Answer**
May I come in, sir?	Yes, you may.
May I use your shirt?	No, you may not.
May I put the television on?	Of course you may.
May I have a look at those photos, please?	Certainly
May I have a word with you in private, please	Oh, sure

- **Might I ?**

This is the most hesitant, polite and respectful way of making a request, but it is hardly use in everyday speech.

Look at the examples :

Questions	**Answer**
Might I borrow your pen, please?	Sure!
Might I make a suggestion?	By all means
Might I use your umbrella	of course, you can.

❑❑❑

Unit-12 Expressing Possibility
(संभावना व्यक्त करना)

Uses of May/Might/Could

The words given above can be used to express present and future possibility.

May : expresses 'possibility' which is almost certain.

Look at the examples :

- The police **may** arrive at any moment; let's run away.
- It **may** rain today. You'd **better** take an umbrella.
- You ought to buy now, prices may go up (in near future).
- Where's Moni? She **may** be with her mother

Negative possibility

- He **may not** be in his office/you **may not** find her at home.
- The president **may not** attend the function today.
- He **may not** be available for talks.

'Can' is very close to 'May' in the affirmative

Here are some examples :

1. You **can/may** qualify the test easily. They can/may raid the house.
2. The government **can/may** grant financial help to charitable hospitals.
3. The police **can/may** tow away your car if you leave it there. (Tow = Pull)
4. Your presence of mind **can/may** save you in dangerous situations.
5. You **may/can** change this train at Delhi. You **can't** reach there directly.

Note : The negative of 'May' is "can't". (Not Mayn't)

In the passive voice 'May' is preferred to 'can' e.g. :

Applications for this post **may** be obtained on request.

Might : shows uncertainty; distant possibility.

Compare :

- I **might** see you tomorrow. (Possible but not 'certain')
- I **may** see you tomorrow. (Suggests strong possibility)

Examples showing element of uncertainty :

- I **might** come and visit you in Delhi some time in June this year.

- India might win the next world cup/he **might** get a job soon.
- If you bought a lottery ticket, you **might** win a luxury car.

He **might not** be available for comments on this point.

A : Is he going to the cinema tonight?

B : he **might** or **might not**. (The speaker is not sure)

■ Could : suggests that something is 'just possible'

Look at the example :

- Most accidents **could** be prevented if the traffic rules are strictly followed.
- You **could** be in a difficult situation if you are not careful.
- The phone is ringing; I think it **could** be your mother!

Could we meet again tomorrow? / He **could** answer your questions.

It **could** be dangerous; it **could** be anything. Let's wait and watch.

They **could** arrive at any time.

■ Future possibility with 'could'

'Could' may express possibility; At times 'can' is also possible.

Look at the example :

Could he be at his college? (It is possible)

Could/Can this is true? **Could/Can** this plan be successful?

Could/Can he leave India this week? **Could/Can** you rely on him?

Could he be at home? **Could** they have arrived by tomorrow?

Couldn't she come on Monday? **Couldn't** he be at his office?

■ Must have; can't have .....

'Must have' refers to the possibility in the past.

The negative of 'must have' (in the past) is : Can't have.

Remember : 'Must' and **'can't'** are opposite in meaning.

Look at the examples :

- He **must have** gone away. He **can't have** gone away.
- He **must have** left early. He **can't have** left early.
- You **must have** left your key at home.
- I **can't have** left it at home.
- It **must be** in your pocket, then?
- I'm sure, it **can't be**.

■ Must have been : indicates possibility in the past.

The negative is : "can't have been"

Look at the examples :

- He **must have been** here (but left)
- He **can't have been** here (**Don't say :** he mustn't have been here)
- He **must have been** in this college (as a student, teacher, etc.)
- He **must have been** an engineer (when he was young)
- The children hadn't eaten for hours. They **must have been** hungry.

Negative : They **can't have been** hungry.

Future possibility

Consider these words : May be / Might be

May be : expresses certainty

Look at the examples :

- She may be at college. (It is possible)
- She may not be at college. (= I don't think she can be)
- She can't be at college. ("Can't be" shows disbelief)

Might be : shows uncertainty

Look at the example :

- He might be at home. (Possible, but not certain)
- He mightn't be at home. (suggest uncertainty)
- Mightn't he be at home? Might be I don't know (or) I'm not sure.

Guessing possibility in the past

Look at the use of following construction :

Can't/could have + past participle

Here are some examples :

- It's Sunday. Pinki **can't have gone** to college.
- I think she **could have gone** to the pictures with her friends.

Don't say : 'Picture'

Say : 'Pictures' as you see not one but series of pictures.

Something was possible but did not happen

Use the following construction to express this idea :

Could have + past participle

Look at the examples :

- You could have told me (that) you had invited them. (But you didn't)
- Why did you jump into the river?
- You could have drowned. (It was possible)

- He could easily have solved the problem. (But he couldn't)
- You could have got a job last year. (But you couldn't)

■ Look at the following construction

May/Might have + past participle

Heres are some examples :

- The missing soldier may have been killed. (possible; but we don't know)
- He might have been hurt in the car accident. (possible. but saved)
- She may have had an accident. (Possible; but we don't know)
- I might have told you if you had asked me. (But you did't)
- They may have been held up by a traffic jam. (Possible)

❑❑❑

Unit-13 Giving advice, instructions
(सलाह और अनुदेश देना)

Consider the following words :

Should/ought

'Should' and **'ought'** are used to give advice, but there is a slight difference between the two.

Look at the following examples :

- ### Should
  - You **should** see a doctor/you should wait for the green lights at the crossroads.
  - He **should** apologize for being so rude/you **shouldn't** drink and drive.
  - The rich **shouldn't** laugh at the poor?

- ### Ought (to) :
  'Ought to' is stronger than 'should'.
  It reminds people of their **moral duty, rules** and **regulations**.

  Look at the examples :
  - You **ought** to see the doctor (emphatic)/you **ought** to vote the party of your choice.
  - People **ought** to pay taxes/you **ought** to be ashamed of yourself/you oughtn't drive fast/ **Oughtn't** you to be more careful? (Yes, I ought to)

- **Had better** (= it would be advisable to .....)
  This expression is commonly used in everyday speech and considered stronger than 'should'. it advises people about what they should do, especially to avoid unpleasant situations, problems or danger. Short forms are common in everyday speech, e.g. :
  I had better **(= I'd better)**; we had better **(= We'd better)**; You had better **(= you'd better)** He had better **(= he'd better)**; She had better **(= she'd better)**; they had better **(= they'd better)** etc.

  Look at the examples :
  - I'd better do something. (= I ought to do something)
  - I think you'd better see a doctor. (Indicates urgency)

- I'd better hurry, or I'll be late/you'd better leave at once/we'd better start right now.
- He'd better take medicine and stay in bed/it might rain. They'd better stay home.
- She'd better return home before seven in the evening.

■ **"Had better not" : (Used to warn people of consequences)**

Look at the examples :

- You'd better not miss this opportunity/they'd better not be late for the lecture.
- He'd better not ignore my advice and see the doctor immediately.
- You'd better not complain to the police about it.
- She'd better not take this risk.

Must

used to give strong advice or orders, e.g.

You must stop smoking / she **must** see the doctor / we **must** go now.

- **Must** I wash all these clothes? (= Is it necessary for me to ....)
  Yes, **you must**. (= Yes, it is necessary)
- **Mustn't** (negative of must)
  Say : Must I go home now? No, you **mustn't**.
  Anita **mustn't** stay out late / we **mustn't** disobey our teachers.
- You **mustn't** smoke in the temple.

The use of Am/Is/Are + to

(for instructions and prohibitions)

- You'**re to** deliver these letters before 9 o'clock. (= You must .....)
- **I'm to see** the doctor immediately. (= I must ....)
- He'**s to** go and see his ailing mother before coming here. (= he must ....)
- You'**re not to** tell them anything about it. (= You mustn't tell ....)
- You'**re not to** throw stones at the dogs. (= You mustn't throw ....)
- They'**re not to** request them for money. (= They mustn't .....)

Need

(as regular verb) = require

- you need a lot of patience and hard work to earn money.
- You'll need Rs. 500/- to open your account in this bank.
- He doesn't need much effort to do this work.

Short dialogue :

- Do I need to show my ticket every time?
- (or) No, you don't need to show the ticket every time.

Have to/Must

- 'Have to' suggests : 'there is no choice'.
- 'Have to' is an alternative to 'must', but there is difference between the two :

When the speaker says, "you must do it" meaning.
'The action is necessary from his point of view' hence, must be done.
'Have to' suggests external pressure to do the action.

Look at the examples :

- You **must** polish your boots /All the cadets will have to polish their boots.
- You **must** drive slowly on a crowded street, said his mother.
- You **have to** drive slowly on a crowded street, warned the police officer.
- you **must** get up early to catch the train / I'll have to get up early to catch the train.
- Kaushal **must** work hard to pass the exams / she **has to** pass the exams if she wants a job.

Have got to

'Got to' form is commonly used in everyday speech.
'Got to' can replace **"have to"**.

Look at the examples :

Present say : I have to go (= I've got to go)
I don't have to go. (= Have I got to go?)
Do I have to go? (= Have I got to go?)
Don't I have to go? (= Haven't I got to go?)

He has to go. = (= He's got to go)
He doesn't have to go. (= he hasn't got to go)
Does he have to go? (= Has he got to go?)
Doesn't he have to go? (= Hasn't he got to go)
Compare : He doesn't have to go. (= he needn't go)

Past Say : I had to go.
I hadn't to go. (= I hadn't got to go)
(or) : I didn't have to go.

Had I to go? (= had I got to go?)
(or) Did I have to go?
Hadn't to go? (Hadn't I got to go?)
(or) Didn't I have to go?

Note : In spoken English "Do I have to?" is emphatic; it is, therefore, preferred to "got to" form. Similarly, in the past the negative question "Didn't" have to? is preferred to "hadn't (got) to" form.

- **Future Say :** I will = I'll

I'll have to go.	I won't have to go.
You'll have to go.	You won't have to go.
He'll have to go.	He won't have to go.
Shall/will I have to go?	Won't I have to go?
Will you have to go?	Won't you have to go?
Will he have to go?	Won't he have to go?

- **The following are the present forms :**

A – (you) needn't go. (= you don't need to go)
(You) don't have to go. (= You haven't got to go)
Meaning : "It is not necessary for you to go."

Look at the past forms :

B - Didn't need to / didn't have to
Meaning : "It wasn't necessary, so perhaps not done."

C-**Needn't have + past participle :**
This structure is used to mean :
"It wasn't necessary but done in spite of that"

Look at the examples :

- I didn't need to go there. (So I didn't go)
- I needn't have gone there. (But I did go)

Here are some more examples :

- I didn't need to lock the door. (It was already locked)
- You didn't have to translate it into English. (You wasted your time)
- She didn't need to go to the office yesterday. (It was a holiday)
- Mr. Yogi needn't have gone to the office yesterday. (He wasted his time)
- I didn't need to answer all the questions. (It saved me a lot of trouble)
- I needn't have answered all the questions. (I wasted my time)

- They needn't have jumped over the wall (but they did)

- **You did not do what was expected of you**

The use of : 'should have + past participle'

Example :

A-You should see the doctor. (Advice)

You shuld have seen the doctor. (But you didn't)

- **You did not do what was necessary.**

Ought to have + past participle

Examples :

A - You ought to stop smoking.
You ought to have stopped smoking. (But you didn't)

B - She ought to leave this place before it is dark.
She ought to have left that place before it was dark. (But she didn't)

C - He oughtn't to tell lies.
He oughtn't to have told lies. (But he did)

- **Am/is/are (to) can be used imaginatively in the past**

Look the exmaples :

A - He **is to come** tomorrow :
He **was to have come** yesterday (but he didn't)

B - The guests **are to arrived** at five this evening.
The guests **were to have arrived** at five yesterday evening.

C - We both **are to leave** India soon.
We both **were to have left** India soon.

❑❑❑

Unit-14 Expressing time, date and day
(समय, तिथि और दिन व्यक्त करना)

Common ways of inquiring about time
(समय के बारे में पूछताछ करने के सामान्य तरीके)

There are two ways of requesting someone to ask the time :
(a) What's the time? (b) What time is it?

Consider the following conversation :

Q. : What's the time, Anita?
Ans : I don't know. Ask Manisha.
Q. : What time is it, Manisha?
Ans : It's nine o'clock.
Thank, you.
Q. : Can you tell me the time, please?
Ans : I am sorry, I don't know. Ask Vinod.
Q. : Can you tell me the time, Vinod?
Ans : Yes, it's ten o'clock
Q. : What time will the train arrive?
Ans : I don't know, but may be at six.

■ **Telling the time (समय बताना)**

Half past; a quarter past; a quarter to

Look at the examples :

Q : What's the time? / What time is it?

Ans :
- (It's) a quarter past eight (8:15) / five past ten (5:10)
- (It's) twenty past ten (10:20)/half past ten (10:30)
- (It's) twenty-five to ten (9:35) / a quarter to ten (9:45)
- (It's) five to three (2:55) / ('Minutes' can be omitted here)
- (It's) a minute past two (2:1) / (= one minute past two)

Note : 'Minutes' is often omitted when the number is in : 5, 10, 20, ...

■ **'When .....?'** (Used to inquire about time), e.g. :

When does the Taj Express leave Agra for Delhi?

(At) **What time** does the Raj Express leave Agra ....?

Note : **'At'** is formal and can be omitted.

When does it arrive in Delhi? It arrives at ten.

Which train do you want to catch?

I'll try to get the 10.30. it arrives at platform three.

I've got to be there in time.

What time have you got to come back?

I'll be back home by evening next week.

When's your flight? Tuesday evening.

What time does the film start? At six thirty.

What time does the post office open?

It opens at ten and **closes** at five in the evening.

It isn't **open** on Saturdays and Sundays. (Open : Adj.)

Talking about days, dates etc. (दिन, तारीख इत्यादि के बारे में बातचीत)

Q. : **What's** today?
Ans : It's Sunday today. (= Today's Sunday)
Q. : **What's** the next day?
Ans : It's Monday.
Q. : **What's** tomorrow?
Ans : it's Monday tomorrow.
Q. : **What was** yesterday?
Ans : It was saturday yesterday.
Q. : **What month is** it now?
Ans : It's June.
Q. : **What was** the last month?
Ans : It was May.
Q. : **How many** days are there in June?
Ans : It has thirty days.
There are thirty days in June.

- **Consider the following examples :**

What's the date (today)? **What's** date it is?

It's **the** twelfth of September / It's **the** twenty first of March.

(or) March **the** next month / in June would you be free?

Dated :

This letter was **dated** May 15, 1999.

Thank you for your letter **dated** September 25th.

When were you born?

I was born **on** January **the** third.

Q : **When's** your mother's birthday?

Ans : It's **on the** thirtieth.

Q : **When's** your wife's birthday?

Ans : it's Monday, **the** 22nd of October.

- **Look at these experessions :**

This morning/this afternoon/this evening / tonight

Examples :

- He's coming to Delhi **this** morning.
- We're meeting **over** lunch **this** afternoon.
- They're going to the cinema **this** evening.
- He's arriving **tonight** (= during the night of today)

Say :

Yesterday morning/yesterday afternoon/ Yesterday evening.

Don't say :

Yesterday night, Say : 'last night' instead.

Also : Tomorrow morning/tomorrow afternoon.

Similarly : tomorrow evening/tomorrow night.

Also : Early morning, e.g. : I'd like an **early** morning flight.

Late evening, e.g. : I'd like to go by a **late** evening flight.

- **On/every can be used with the days of the week, e.g.**

He came on Sunday/Monday ..... (+ morning/afternoon, etc.)

Look at the examples :

- He came on Sunday morning / he went **on** Tuesday night.
- I'll see you **on** Friday afternoon, etc.

Say : He comes **on Tuesday (= every tuesday).**

Similarly : She goes on Sundays/Mondays/Tuesdays, etc.

- **Say :** Every morning/every afternoon/every evening .... e.g. :

He used to exercise **every** morning/they drank **every** evening.

He visited her quitely **every** night.

Note : 'every' refers to 'frequency'. It means :

Somebody did something **every** (= each) day/morning, etc.

- **Say :** One summer morning/**one** warm summer evening.

One morning/**last** week.

Likewise : On a cold night/on a hot night/on a winter's night/on a wet night ...., etc.

Look at the examples :

He died **on the morning** of May the first / I was born **on the night of** 15th of August.

He left home **on the evening of** Saturday, **the** 15th of June 1968.

Week/Weekend/fortnight (सप्ताह/सप्ताहांत/पखवाड़ा)

Week : a period of seven days, e.g. :

Sunday is the **first** day of the **week**. The **last** day of the **week** is **Saturday**.

Weekend/Weekends : a weekend is Saturday.

Note : in theWest people don't go to work or school **at** weekend.

Look at the examples :

Cinema halls are full **at** weekends/What do you do **at** weekend?

Fortnight : a **period** of **two** weeks, e.g. :

They're staying in Delhi for a fortnight/he met me a fortnight ago.

❑❑❑

Unit-15 Making Telephone Calls
(टेलीफोन कॉल करना)

Look at the examples :

- He said he would **phone me** tomorrow/she phoned me whether I was free.
- I"ll telephone him this evening/he phoned the hospital to ask if she was OK.
- Please **phone 100** if you need police assistance/she telephoned to thank me.
- Will you please **phone up** "Enquiries" for information?

Words and phrases used to make phone calls
(फोन कॉल करने के लिए उपयोग किये जाने वाले शब्द और वाक्यांश)

▪ **Ring (v) :** to make a telephone call to someone, e.g.

- He **rang** me twice this morning / I **rang** him but he wasn't in.
- She **rang** you at about nine o'clock last night.
- Shall I **ring** for a taxi? Please **ring** 100 for police assistance.
- You must **ring** the doctor immediately.
- Ring (n) : a cll, eg. I gave him **a ring** last night.
- I'll give you **a ring** this evening (= telephone you)
- can I give you a ring in case I need you?

◆ **Ring up (Informal) :** to telephone someone, e.g.

- She **rang up** while I was out/I'll **ring** you **up** tomorrow.
- Why don't you **ring up** the police?/She just **rang** me **up**.

◆ **Ring off :** to end a phone call, e.g. :

- She **rang off** after giving me the news / he howled and **rang off**.
- He insisted but she said, "No, than you" and **rang off**.

◆ **Ring back :** to phone again, e.g.

- Please **ring back** later /I'll **ring back** in the evening. I'm busy now.
- Can I **ring** you **back** in about half an hour? Of course , you can.

▪ **Call (v) : to phone someone, e.g.**

- Hello, who's calling? / She **called** me this morning but I wasn't home.

- Shall I **call** the doctor? Who **called** you this morning.
- **Call** me when you get home/I'll call you tonight

◆ **Call back : ring back, e.g.**

- Ask him to **call** me **back** when he gets in / I'm busy; can **I call** you **back** later?
- **Call** (n) : I'll give you a **call** tomorrow / he didn't answer my **call**.
- I've got three **phone calls** since morning / Were there any phone calls for me?

■ **Call up (Am Eng)/informal :**

- I'll call you **up** this evening / **call** me **up** at any time.
- I **called** you **up** this morning, but nobody answered the phone.
- My father **called** me **up** from his office.

■ **Call in : to make a phone call to help.**

(or) : to phone someone where you work.

Look at the examples :

- They **called in** the police to control the rowdy group of students.
- She called in to say she'd be late by half an hour. (**'d** = would)

■ **Learn the following words and expressions**

(a) Dialling/dial tone : The sound produced by a telephone when you pick up the receiver.

(b) Dialling code : A short group of numbers used before dialling a particular number, e.g. - 011 is the dialling code for Delhi.

(c) Secret code : A digital locking facility to keep effective control over the STD/ISD calls.

(d) Extension (number) : A telephone connected to the switchboard of a company or institution, e.g.
Call me at the company extension 1204/ Call me at 2.30; I'm on extension 329.

(e) Ring : When a telephone ring, it makes a sound, e.g.
The phone is ringing/the phone rang about two o'clock.
Didn't the phone ring last night.

(g) Answer the phone please. (= Pick up the telephone)
When a telephone rings, you pick up the receiver to answer it, e.g.

- The phone is ringing; answer the phone please.
- The phone was ringing. As I was going to answer it, it stopped.
- Let me answer the phone; it must be from my boss.

(h) Wrong number : You say, "Wrong number" when your phone call is connected to some other phone by mistake, e.g.
- She often dials the wrong number.
- Sorry, you have the wrong number.
- I think you've got the worng number; this is 123945
- It was just a wrong number.

(i) A dead telephone : A phone is dead if it has no electrical power, e.g. The phone has gone dead.

(j) Held up : The phone is 'held up' meaning :
It has jammed due to some mechanical fault.

(k) Hold the line/hold on : used to say
"Please wait for a moment." (= Don't put the phone down)
Examples : Could I speak to Moni? Please hold on I'm calling her.

How to use the following expressions

(a) On the phone : making a telephone call, eg :
- He told me about the accident on the phone/he spoke to me on the telephone.
- While I was on the phone somebody knocked at the door.
- Dad, you'are on the telephone.

(b) Over the phone : by means of, e.g.
- Be careful! Someone's listening to our conversations over the phone.
- I'm sorry; I can't discuss this matter over the phone, please.
- He spoke to me over the phone.

(c) By phone : by means of (using the telephone), e.g. :
- He called the police by phone / I booked two tickets to London by phone.
- She can be contacted by phone/we received the message by phone.

Speaking to someone on the phone

Say : Hello!
Can I speak to Raju, Please (Informal)
Raju : Oh, hello, guy! How are you?

Here are some examples :
- This is ..... (Say when introducing yourself)
- Hello, this is Vinod speaking. Can I speak to Pooja, please.

Pooja : Hi, Vinod, this is Pooja, here.
Vinod : Oh, hello, Pooja. Can you meet me at seven this evening?

Pooja : Fine. See you then, bye-bye!

Manoj : Hello, can I speak to Mr. Rajeev, please?

Mr. Rajeev : Yes speaking.

Manoj : Good morning. This is Mukesh from Delhi.

Mukesh : Hello, is that 297650?

Dr. Ghosh : Yes. Who's speaking, please?

Mukesh : this is Mukesh from Hindu Rao Hospital.

Priyanka : Hello, this is Dr. Sonal from S. N. Hospital.

Dr. Roy : Oh, hello Sonal, How are you?

Sonal : fine, thanks.

❑❑❑

Unit-16 Asking the Way
(रास्ता पूछना)

- What will you do if you **"Get lost?"** (= unable to find your way)
Perhaps, you would request someone to show you the right way.
How would you make a request someone to show you the right way.
Asking the way (रास्ता पूछना)

Look at these examples :

• **Can you** tell me the way to the station? (Informal)
• (Or) **Do you** know the way to the station?

- **Making a request for direction** (दिशा बताने के लिए अनुरोध करना)
Could you direct me to the station? (= Will you please ...?)
Can you direct me to the station, **Please?** (= a polite request)
The request can be more polite if you add : "Would you ...?'

Look at the examples :

Excuse me, **would you** mind directing me to the station?
Would you **kindly** show me the way to the airport?

- **If asking about a particular road** (अगर किसी विशेष सड़क के बारे में पूछ रहे हैं)
Say : Do you know the road that goes to the station?
Which road goes to the airport?
Where does this road go? The answer could be :
(Pointing) This road goes to the station.
The road **next to** the church goes to the airport.
Do you see that road? It goes **direct** to Dehli.

- **Words and phrases used to give direction**
(दिशा-निर्देश देने में प्रयुक्त शब्द/वाक्यांश)
Near/by/beside/by the side of/close/next (to)
Note : These words nearly express the same meaning.
The choice depends on the meaning you wish to express.

Words/phrases showing position, motion and direction.
(स्थिति, गति और दिशा दिखाने वाले शब्द/वाक्यांश)

In : in a place or area; surrounded by
Into : shows motion inward (towards the inside)
In the north of : in the northern part of an area or country
At : indicates position or place (where someone or something is)
For example : **at** Delhi; **at** the restaurant, etc.

Look at the example :

- My office is **in the North of** Delhi.
- It's **at** 75 MG Road, a ten-minute drive from here.
- If you want to see me there, follow the instructions :
- Drive straight; **turn right into** Subhash Street and then **turn left**.
- Drive straight till you arrive **at** Green Park Colony.
- There's a Chinese restaurant

Here are some more words and phrases :

Past : by (= go from one side of a person/place or thing to the other)

Examples :

- He goes past (= by) the post office every morning on his way to work.
- He drove past the church/they went past the road to my village.

Towards (की ओर) : In the direction of, eg. :

- Go straight **towards** the station and **turn right**.
- Go **along** this road; **turn into** Gali No 4 and then walk **towards** the bridge.
- He took a **wrong turn** and began driving **towards** the east.

Beyond (के परे) : On the other side of, eg :

His house is **beyond** the station/don't go **beyond** the park.
Beyond the street (on the farther side of the street) there's a shopping mall.

Off (दूर, से दूर) (away from)

We saw a narrow lane off (= branching from) the main road.
His house is off the road (= away from the road)

Over/round/across (के ऊपर/ चारों ओर / पार करना)

'Over' is used to show a path or road going up and the down, 'round' shows a path moving on a sides of something and 'across' means : on the opposite side of.

Look at the examples :

- The path goes **through** a wood, **over** a bridge, **round** a hill and **across** a railway line.
- The bridge goes **over** the river. (**Opp :** 'under the bridge')

On (पर)

Refers to the upper surface, eg : **On** a hill/floor, etc.

I met her on the street.

It also indicates : **nearness** or **next** to, eg :

- My house is **on** the the main road (= very close to). She lives **on** Marine Drive.
- My village is **on** the road from Tundla to Agra/Delhi is **on** the river Jamuna.
- There is a small village **on the border** of Indian and Pakistan.
- He lives **in** a town **on** the cost.

On the left/ on the right (of)

Examples :

There's a Mall **on the left** and a bank **on the right of** my office.

In the middle of, eg :

I saw a roundabout **in the middle of** the road.

Examples :

- There's a teashop **in front of** the cinema.
- There's barber's (shop) **at the back of** it.
- There's a pond **at the back of** (= behind) my house.

Opposite (विपरीत)

- facing; on the other side of, eg :
- Excuse me, Where's the post office?
- It's just **opposite** the tall building.
- it's in the MG Road, **opposite** the bank.

▪ Inside/outside/on the top of/at the top of/round the corner

Look at the examples :

She's inside the hotel and her husband's **outside** the hotel.

- **On the top of :** (= on the highest part of) :.
- **Opposite :** at the bottom of, eg :
  There's a car park **at the bottom of** the tall building.
- **Below :** My office is **on the top floor**. There's another office **below** it

He lives in the flat **below** mine. (**Opposite :** above)

- **Round the corner :** Very near the corner; very nearby, eg :
  I live just **round the corner**/there's shop **round the corner**.

Conversations (वार्तालाप)

Sumit : (to the policeman)
We want to go to this address, please.

Policeman : It's a very **long way** from here, but anyway :
Go straight, about two kilometers from here, and then **turn right**.
After a short walk, **turn left**. That's M. G. Road.
Take the first street **on the right** and the second **on the left**.
The place is **at the end of** the street.

At the airport (हवाई अड्डे पर)

Moni : Can you tell me **the way to** Sough Avenue, please?

Guide : When you leave this building **go straight** and then turn left. Turn **right off** the main road into a narrow lane; walk along **up to** the University Road; cross the railway line and go **past** the Regal Cinema. Then **turn left**; go ahead **towards** the park. South venue is just **next to** it.

Learn these words and expressions

Get : reach; **calling :** phoning; **get down :** alight (get out of)
Crossroads : a place where two roads cross each other.
Wayside : roadside; **move ahead :** move forward.
Forks (v) : divides into two parts
Fork (n) : the point where a road divides into two parts.
Winds : moves in a curve; **go down :** go along.
Bend (n) : a curve; **a sharp bend :** a sharp curve/turn.

- ## Giving directions on the phone (फोन से दिशा बताना)

Rajesh : Hi, Kanika!
Kanika : Can you tell me how to get to your house?
In fact, I've no idea where you live. (Get = Reach)
Rajesh : Where are you at the moment?
Kanika : I'm **calling** you from outside the Youth hostel.

Rajesh : All right. Now listen carefully and follow the instructions :

Well, take an auto and reach the main road; get **down** at the mall.

Walk **through** the busy road and **arrive at** the first crossroads. **Rajesh** : Do you follow me?

Kanika : Oh, yes.

Rajesh : Now, continue walking along the road towards the east until you **arrive at** another crossroads; **turn right** and **walk along** until you **arrive at a wayside** 'Dhaba'.

Kanika : OK. What to do next?

Rajesh : Well, move **ahead** until you reach the bridge; the road **forks** here; take the right hand **fork**. The road **winds** through a small village. Go **down** the road and just before taking the **turning** to the left you'll see a **sharp bend** in the road. A few yards away from here you'll see a big house. That's where I live.

Kanika : O God! See you then, bye!

❑❑❑

Unit-17 Feelings and Emotions
(भावनाएँ और उमंगें)

- **Congratulating people** (लोगों को बधाई देना)

When you congratulate someone you express your pleasure and approval. The occasion could be any : the birth of a child; someone's engagement, marriage, winning a prize, coming first, good sense and wise decision, promotion, appointment, nomination, election or any such thing.

Congratulate (on) :

Means you look at someone with pleasure, praise or respect.

Look at the examples :

- They came to congratulate Mr and Mrs Simon.
- Congratulations on your marriage! Many congratulations to you!

Response : Thank you/thank you very much/thanks a **lot**.

Sumit : Congratulations on your success!

Moni : Thank you. I've passed my exams.

Look at these as well :

A : I got my appointment letter yesterday.

B : Thanks for your compliments!

A : Thank you.

B : Please give Monika my congratulations when you see her.

A : I will.

- **Giving and receiving compliments**

(मुबारकबाद/बधाई देना और प्राप्त करना)

Compliment : an expression of praise, approval or respect

Compliments (Plural) : Expression of appreciation or respect

Look at the examples :

A : The dinner was excellent. My compliments to your wife !

B : Thanks for your compliments !

A : You're looking very smart in your new grey suit.

B : Oh, thank you for showering me with compliments !

▪ Compliment (अभिवादन/प्रशंसा)

Mr Yogi paid his wife a well-deserved compliment.
I always take my boss's criticism as a compliment.
She blushed at the compliment when I said :
"I like your rosy cheeks, my love!"

▪ Compliment (on) :

You compliment someone on his success, performance, etc.

Look at the examples :

- He Complimented Manisha on her superb performance at the dance competition.
- I complimented the police officer on his handling a very difficult situation.
- The police officer was complimented for handling the situation so well.

▪ Complimenting on possessing something, eg :
(कुछ रखने पर तारीफ करना)

- He complimented his neighbour on his new car.
- She complimented me on my new dress.
- I complimented her on her new hairstyle.

▪ People celebrate anniversary/anniversaries :
(लोग सालगिरह/वार्षिकोत्सव मनाते हैं :)

Anniversary is a day or date that people celebrate because on this day something important happened in a previous year, eg : You celebrate a birth anniversary, wedding anniversary, etc. You celebrate anniversaries of particular events, eg; They celebrated the fiftienth anniversary of their country's independence yesterday.

▪ Birthday greetings (good wishes) (जन्मदिन का अभिवादन)

What to say when greeting someone on his/her birthday.

Say : Happy birthday to you!
Happy birthday, my dear!
Happy returns of the day!
Response : Thank you / thank you very much

▪ Special occasions : (विशिष्ट/खास अभिवादन)

People celebrate **silver jubilee** of their marriage; you celebrate **golden jubilee** of your college; your grandfather celebrated **diamond jublee** of your college; your grandfather celebrated **diamond jubilee** of his birth last year.

Note : A jubilee is the celebration of a special anniversary of some event.

- **Silver jubilee, Golden jubilee, Diamond jubilee**

Silver jubilee : (the 25th anniversary), eg;
My congratulations on the silver jubilee of your marriage!
Response : Thank you! / thank you very much!
And thanks a lot for the wedding present.

Golden Jubilee (the 50th anniversary)
Congratulate someone on the Golden jubilee of his/her birth.

Diamond Jubilee (the 60th anniversary) :
This is celebrated exactly after sixty years of one's birth or marriage, eg
I congratulated his grandfather on the **diamond jubilee** of his birth.
Mr. Sethi : "Please give him my congratulations on his diamond wedding".

- **Wishing on a happy occasion :** (शुभ अवसर पर अभिवादन)

Say : merry Christmas !
Wish you a merry Christmas and a Happy New Year !
Wish you a happy and prosperous Deepawali!
Response : Thank you, the same to you.

- **For a safe journey** (सुरक्षित यात्रा के लिए)

Say : Wish you a safe journey!
'Wish you a happy journey'.
Response : thank you.

If you are wishing someone success (अगर आप किसी की सफलता की कामना कर रहे हैं)

Say : Wish you good luck! / Good luck to you! best of luck !
I wish you the best of luck in / with your exams, etc. !
Response : Thank you.

- **All the best !** (शुभकामनाएँ) (= I wish you all success!)

(Or) I hope everything will go well with you.
Response : Thank you.

- **God bless you!** (भगवान आपका भला करे) (An expression of good wishes)

Say this to thank someone for his kind act, eg :
Let me show you the way, sir .....
Response : God bless you, my dear !

Also : used to express affection/good wishes to someone, eg : God bless you! it's very nice of you to come here to see me.

Response : Thank you.

- **Do your best! (पूरी ताकत से करना).** (= Try as hard as you can)

You say this to encourage someone for achieving something difficult.

Response can be : I/we will.

- **If you are showing sympathy (अगर आप सहानुभूति दिखा रहे हैं)**

Say : Bad luck! Oh, bad luck! / I'm terribly sorry!

(Terribly = very/extremely)

- **Expressing a desire or hope (इच्छा या आशा व्यक्त करना)**

Desire : May all your wishes come true! May God bless you!

Hope : We hope and pray that she will recover!

You're quite well, I hope!

I hope you don't mind my saying this, but I don't like your spitting!Hope for the best! Will he come back? We sincerely hope so!You'll be home at six? I hope so!

I hope I didn't wake you!

You'are our only hope now! / He's the hope of the family!

- **Expressing surprise (आश्चर्य व्यक्त करना)**

Look at these words : fantastic, incredible, amazing.

They are used to describe something strange or very difficult to believe, eg.

You went to see:	**Your immediate reaction:**
Taj Mahal in the moonlit night!	**How fantastic!** (= How wonderful)
You saw : A chimpanzee playing the guitar!	**Incredible!** (= I can't believe it)
You saw in your dream : A fairy with wings!	**Amazing!** (= incredible)

Words showing strong feelings and emotions (प्रबल भावनाओं और उमंगों को दर्शाने वाले शब्द)

- **Wow!/Gosh! (वाह!/भगवान!)**

The words given above show how surprised you are, eg :

Gosh, I never thought of you to be here!
One million! Gosh that's incredible!
Wow! Did you make this doll? It's beautiful!

- **My goodness! (हे भगवान)**
  Used to show surprise or anger, eg :
  My goodness! You've finished everything!
- **Good Heavens! (अरे या वाह)**
  Used to express surprise or annoyance, eg :
  Good heavens! What a mess! (= Dirty/disorderly state)
- **O God!/My God! (हे भगवान!/हे भगवान!)**
  Used to express surprise/show emphasis, eg :
  O God! They're coming here right now.
  My God, I,ve forgotten to lock the door!
- **For God's sake! (भगवान/खुदा के लिए)**
  Used to draw attention, eg :
  For God's sake don't talk about him!
- **Thank God! (धन्यवाद भगवान)**
  You feel relaxed (the trouble is over), eg :
  Thank God! We're safe now.

- **Hell (नरक) : a strong expression, eg :**
  Go to hell! (= Go away!)
  I'm tried of you; go to **hell**! / Oh, go to **hell**!
  Oh **hell**! I've left my umbrella somewhere.

- **Expressing strong feelings of annoyance or surprise**
  (झुंझलाहट या आश्चर्य की तीव्र भावनाओं को व्यक्त करना)
  Look at the example :
  What the hell are you talking about?
  What the hell are you doing in my room?
  How the hell are we going to settle this problem?
  How the hell does she think she is ?
  To hell with : (used to say that you don't care at all), eg :
  To hell with this job! I'm going to leave this and get another one.

■ Expressing sudden emotions/strong feelings

(आकस्मिक संवेग/दृढ़ भावनाओं को व्यक्त करना)

Look at the examples :

What a beautiful weather! / What a horrible weather! (= very bad)

How **lovely** you look! What a lovely **baby**! (= Beautiful/attractive)

What a **lovely** house! / What a **lovely** evening! (= Pleasant and enjoyable)

What a **lovely** flower! / What a **lovely** surprise! (= Wonderful)

How **beautifully** you sing! / What a **rude** man! (= Not showing respect)

What a **fuss** she made! (= Unnecessary nervous excitment)

How **awful**! / How **awful** weather! ! The food **smells** awful! (= Very bad)

What a **dreadful** woman she is! (Of very low quality)

How **madly** he drives! / What an idiot! (Idiot = fool)

❑❑❑

Unit-18 Routine activities
(नियमित गतिविधियाँ)

- The following words refers to place where you go to relieve (urinate) yourself or get rid of waste matter from your body :

Toilet, Lavatory, Latrine, Washroom, Bathroom urinal, Loo and Toilet :

A toilet is a room with a large bowl that you sit on to get rid of urine or waste matter from your body.

Say : Go to the **toilet** (With 'the')

Look at the examples :

I want to go to the **toilet**. He's (= he has) just gone to the **toilet**. She's in the **toilet**.

Could I use your **toilet**? Where's the **toilet**? You must flush the **toilet** after using it.

- **Flush the toilet** (शौचालय में फ्लश चलाना)

You press the handle of a toilet to wash it away with a rush of water, eg :

Flush the toilet's blocked you try **flushing** it out with hot water; you say :

I've tried **flushing** it several times but it's still blocked.

Lavatory (old-fashioned) : a lavatory is the same as a toilet, eg.

I want to go to **the lavatory**.

Public lavatories : toilets for people in general.

Latrine : a common word for 'toilet' in India.

Note : People in rural India usually defecate in the open.

Defecate : to get rid of waste matter from the bowels.

Wash-room : (An English) a room with toilets, eg :

I want to go to the **wash-room** / she in the **wash-room**.

Is there a **wash-room** near here?

- **Bathroom** (स्नानगृह)

Bathroom is a place where people take a bath. it also contains a toilet.

Go to the bathroom (= use a toilet), eg. I want to go to the bathroom.

Look at these examples :

- Can I go to the **bathroom** to take a bath (= wash himself)
- Can you tell me where the bathroom (= toilet) is?

1. **Urinal :** a round container fitted to a wall for men to urinate in.
2. **Urinal :** refers to a **building** containing urinals for men to urinate in, eg;

   There's a urinal next to the library.

Public urinal : a building in a public place with several urinals for men.

Loo (informal) a toilet.

Look at the example

- Where's Sania? I think she's in the **Loo**/I want to go to the **Loo**.
- **The ladies' Loos** are upstairs/there's a **Loo** on the first floor.
- Could you tell me where **the Loo** is?

■ **Public conveniences :** in British English 'Convenience' refers to a toilet.

Public conveniences are provided in a public place for people to use them.

The toilet for the use of men are called : **(a) The Gents** (= Men's toilets)

The toilets for women are called : **(b) The ladies** (= Women's) toilets

Here are some examples :

Excuse me, Where's The Gents?

Can you tell me where the Gents is?

The ladies :

Examples : Could you direct me to **the Ladies' toilets**, please?

(Or) : Can you tell me where **The ladies is**?

I want to go to **The Ladies,** please.

Is there **a ladies** near here?

❑❑❑

Unit-19 Visiting the Doctor
(डॉक्टर के पास जाना)

▪ Common complaints (आम शिकायतें)

Most people **go to the doctor's** (clinic) for minor illnesses like, fever, cold, aches and pains, etc. Consider the following conversation between a doctor and his patient:

Doctor : How are you feeling?
Patient : Not well, doctor. When I woke up this morning? I wasn't feeling well.
Doctor : Let me take your pulse (= feel the pulse)
Patient : I've got a fever and coughing often.
Doctor : Since when?
Patient : Since last night.
Doctor : Let me take your temperature. You're a bit feverish (= having a slight fever) Don't worry! Your trouble is a minor illness, just a mild cold.
Patient : I'm sneezing repeatedly; I think I'm allergic to cold.
Doctor : I think so. You've got all the symptoms of a cold : the cough, sneezes and the sore throat. but anyway, take this medicine right now, it'll help the fever go down; drink plenty of liquids and stay indoors to keep yourself warm.

▪ Have (got)

If you have or get an illness, injury or pain you suffer from it, eg.

I **have** a fever.

(Or) **I've got** a fever.

Remember : 'have got' is basically a perfect form.

Use 'had' in the past. ('Had got' is not preferred)

'Didn't have' is the negative form. ('Hadn't got' is not preferred)

'Did (you) **have ....?'** is the commonest form in past questions.

Look at the following examples :

- He's got a toothache/she's **got** severe abdominal pains.
- I'm not going to the office today. **I've got** a fever.

Didn't you **have** a toothache last week?

Yes, **I got** (= had) a severe pain on Monday last.

Note : 'have' and **'have got'** are used to describe **pains** and **illnesses**. **'Have got'** is a british expression; in American English people use, 'have' instead.

As for habitual disease, **'have'** is a commonly used expression, eg.

- He's got a fever and a sore throat. (Present reference)
- I usually **have** colds in winter. (Tendency)
- Do you often **have** constipation? (Habit)

Here are some more examples :

- She hasn't much fever but her daughter **has/she's got** a high fever.
- You'll **get** (= feel) cold if you don't wear warm clothes.
- I **got** a cold (= the illness) form exposure / she's **got** a bad backache.
- When you **have** (= catch) a cold your nose is blocked and you sneeze a lot.
- **I've got** a cold and a slight fever/Monika's got a sore throat.
- My father's **got** a stomachache and my mother's **got** a headache.
- She's **got** a terrible (= bad) cough / the man **had** a severe cough every winter.

The use of a/an with illnesses

The indefinite article 'a' is used with common diseases like : fever/cough/cold/headache/sore throat, eg.

- My nose runs when **I have /got/caught** a cold.
- She's got a terrible (= very bad) cough/he's got a slight headache.
- Do you have a sore throat? / I've got a fever/he's in bed with a high fever, etc.

Have a backache/stomachache/toothache, eg.

- I have a slight ache in my lower back/she had **an** earache.

Don't use article with disease which are **plural** in form such as : measles/ mumps, eg :

I had mumps last years/she's got measles, etc.

Technical names of diseases such as : diabetes, cancer, aids, tuberculosis, blood pressure, malaria, flu, gout, hepatitis, etc. do not take article with them.

Say : Cancer is a serious disease/he's got appendicitis/my children are in bed with influenza for five days, etc.

Describing causes and symptoms (कारणों और लक्षणों का वर्णन)

What caused you fever?

I got it from exposure/exposure to dry, cold wind.

The fever **came on** from intense cold/intense heat.

The fever **came on** form having been out in the cold wind/from the intensely hot weather / the fever **came on** high /it began with shivering and chills/I had thirst for cold water. The attack **came on** in the night/ after exposure/early in the evening/it **came on** after taking cold during the day/I went out in **cold air** with my light clothing and **came down** (= collapsed)

Conversation (वार्तालाप)

Doctor : **What's wrong with you?**

Patient : I've got a fever and feeling **a good deal of** (= a lot of) pain and **shortness** of breath. Please, give me some medicine to make my **breathing** easier.

Doctor : **How did you get it?**

Patient : A slight cold made me sick. yesterday I got **exposed** to the cold wind. The fever came on high; it **downed** me with a **wheezing** (= shistling/hissing sound in the chest). I felt much sneezing without relief, **sweated** with intense thirst, **anxiety** and **restlessness;** I felt **giddy** on rising. I'm feeling much **tired** and **breathless** at the moment.

The inflammation of the throat (गले की सूजन) Inflammation :

the painful redness/swelling

Patient : please look into my throat.

There's acute (= very severe and sharp) pain and swelling in the throat and I'm feeling **extreme** pain in **Swallowing** things, even liquids; coughing up (= clearing) **Phlegm** (= the thick yellowish substance) is difficult and painful; I've got **headache** and **pain** in the back and limbs.

Doctor : Let me first examine your throat : open your mouth wide and push your tongue forward. **Oh, how dreadful!** (Dreadful : very bad) The back of your mouth's red and **dry**; cough made **breathing** difficult.

A bad cough (बुरी खांसी)

When you catch a cold in dry, cold air several severe symptoms come up.

You go to the clinic and say :

Doctor, I've got a **terrible** (= serious) cough!

I'm **breathing** with difficulty; feeling **soreness** of cough with a **wheezing** sound in the chest with **feverish** heat; it gets **worse** in the evening/ when **lying down;** cold food, cold drinks and cold air **aggravate** (= worsen) the symptoms; I feel very **uncomfortable** (= oppressive) when going **upstairs**; severe fits of **cough** and **suffocation** force me to **sit up** when the attack **comes** on it **shakes** the whole body; it's followed by **sneezing** and **running** of the nose; a thick, **sticky** liquid (= irritating sensation) in the throat. Since last night I've been suffering from **hoarseness** and **severe** pain in the head.

Note : 'hoarseness' refers to the roughness in sound.

- **Talking about aches and pains** (दर्द एवं पीड़ा के बारे में बातचीत)

(At the clinic)

Patient : I'm in pain, doctor!

Doctor : Let me examine you first. All right, now answer my questions :

What's causing you pain?Where do you feel it?

What's the pain like? (= What sort of pain is it?)

When did it start? how often do you **have** it, and how long?

What makes it **worse?** Is it your first chance you've got it?

Can you show me the exact place where you **have** it?

Does it come or go? When do you feel it most?

Is there anything that **relieves** you of the pain?

- **People suffer from** (लोग पीड़ित हैं)

headache/toothache/earache/backache/stomachache

Old people usually have : aching in the limbs/pain in the lower part of the back/pains of the joints and muscles.

You **have** pains from **bruises/injuries** or when you fall down and **sprain** your **ankle,** etc.

Pains can be :

Dull (= annoying but not very painful); **intense** (= felt very strongly)

Violent (= very painful and difficult to control)

(Be) in pain/feel pain/have a pain, eg :

Take this capsule if you're **in** pain (= having a pain)

If you're **feeling** pain in the chest, **see** the doctor immediately.

- **Aggravates** (गंभीरता बढ़ाना) **:** (= becomes more serious)

Say : The pain **aggravates** by cold/by coughing/by eating/by walking.

When does it aggravate?

it aggravates **in** the morning/**during** the night/**at** midnight.

It's worse **in open** air/**much worse** in the morning **on rising.**

Get worse (= become more serious) **(बढ़ जाना)**

The pain gets **worse** in the morning/after getting **out of bed**.

The pain gets **much worse** in the daytime.

I feel better :

I feel better by walking/in the fresh air/after eating/during the night.

- **Types of pain :** (पीड़ा के प्रकार)

Bursting/shooting/cutting/stabbing/stinging/tearing/rending/burning/Stiching/cramping/pressing/boring/throbbing (=pulsating)

◆ **Bursting pains :** a bursting pain is a sudden strong pain that lasts for a short time; it has too much pressure inside; **shooting pains** are sudden sharp pains (the patient is oversensitive to pain in this condition), eg : Shooting pain in the back/teeth/abdomen, etc.

Cutting pains are knife-like; **stabbing pain** are sharp and sudden as if being stabbned, eg.

- Stabbing headaches/stabbing pains in the back, etc.

◆ **Stinging pain** (pricking pain) is sharp like the bite of an insect, eg;

- I'm feeling stinging pain in my head.
- When pains are **tearing** or **rending,** it is serious enough (damaging muscles).
- You feel as if a part of your body were being torn or ripped apart violently.
- You complain of tearing pain in the brain, in temples and head; **burning pain** causes burning sensation, eg. I felt burning pain in my stomach after eating.

◆ **Stitching pain :** you feel as if needles were being pushed in and out, eg; I fellt stitching pain in the head/stiching pain in the chest.

◆ **Cramp** is severe pain caused by sudden **tightening** of a **muscle**; it makes movement difficult. **eg :**

- He suddenly got (a) cramp like dull pain in the temples.
- She had the cramp in her leg, etc.

◆ **Pressing pain :** eg : After eating, I felt pressing pain in my stomach; if you feel **boring pain**, you feel like someone making holes, eg; She had deep boring pains in the forehead.

◆ **Throbbing pain :** If you have a throbbing pain, you feel strong beats like pain.

You say : the throbbing pain in my head is becoming unbearable/his wound throbbed with pain, etc.

❑❑❑

Unit-20 Pointing to People and Things

(लोगों और चीजों की ओर इशारा करते हुए)

- **Use of demonstratives** (संकेतात्मक प्रयोग)

  Don't say : He's my friend/she's my sister/it's my pen, etc. When **pointing** to people and things. **The reason :** he, she and it are **subject pronouns** and as such can be used only in place of **noun subject**; as for showing someone or something by pointing at, the correct way is to use the **demonstratives** instead. **These are :** this, that, these, those.

- **Expressing nearness** (निकटता व्यक्त करना)

  Use 'this' for **people** and **things** that are very **close** (near) to you, eg.
  This is John. (**Don't say :** He is John)
  This is my purse. (**Not :** It is my purse).
  Note : the plural of 'this' is **'these'**.

  Look at these examples :

  Hello, I'm John from the United States.
  This is my friend, Amit. (= **Here's** my friend, Amit)
  This is my passport. (= **here's** my passport)
  And **these** are my suitcases. (= **Here** are my suitcases)
  Note : **'this'** and **'these'** can be associated with 'here'.

This/These

Look at these examples :

- **This** is my table. (**Don't say :** It is .....)
  It's made of wood.
- **These** are my shoes. (**Not :** They're ....)
  They're made of leather.
- Are **these** your dolls? (**Not :** They're ....?)

Look at these too :

- This is Juhi. She's a student. **This** is Monu. He's my son.
- **These** are boys and girls. They're my classmates. **These** are toys.
- They're made in China. **This** is my coffee. **It** suits my taste.
- **This** is your milk. it's the skimmed milk. Are **these** eggs for me?

■ Expressing distance (दूरी व्यक्त करना)

'That' is used to show someone/something at a **distance**.
The plural of **'that'** is **'those'**.
Note : 'that' and 'those' can be associated with **'there'**.
Examples :
That's Sonu/**That's** Juhi / **those** are boys.
(**Don't say :** He's/she's/they're ......)

Here are some more examples :

- **That's** my house. It's very bit.
- **Those** are chairs. They're armchairs.

Q. : Who's **that**?
Ans : **That's** Ravi, a friend of mine.
Q. : Who are **those** people ?
Ans : They're my parents.
That's my car. it's a racing car.
That's your coat. It's blue in colour.
Q. : What are **those**?
Ans : They're glass animals.
Q. : Do you know **these** guys?
Ans : Yes. They're Mr and Mrs John. (**Don't say :** Mrs and Mr ...)
Q. : Excuse me! Are **those** for sale?
Ans : yes, they are.
Note : demonstratives are replaced by he, she, it and they a second time.

Look at these examples :

- I like **this** shirt. I don't like **that** shirt. **This** bread is **stale** (= not fresh).
- Who are **these** people? Who are **those** men chatting at the traffic lights?
- What are **these** girls doing? Who are **those** women standing over there?
- Don't eat **these** mangoes. They aren't ripe enough. Are **those** toys yours?

■ Asking about place/places where you are:

(आप जहाँ हैं उस स्थान/स्थानों के बारे में पूछना)

Q. : What's **this** place called?
Ans : **This** is Sanjay place.
Q. : Is **this** Connaught place?
Ans : No, It's Chandni Chowk.
Q. : What's **that**? Is **that** a temple?

Ans : Yes. it is.
Q. : What are **these**?
Ans : They are Government Offices.
Q. : What are **those** over there?
Ans : They are apartments.

Going round the city : (शहर का चक्कर लगाना)

- **This** is Delhi University/**that's** parliament House.
- **This** is Women's College/**that's** Ashoka Hotel/**this** is Kutub Minar.
- **Those** are Railway Quarters/**this** is Chandni Chowk.
- Is **that** Parliament House?

▪ Talking about situations and locations
(स्थिति और परिस्थिति के बारे में बातचीत)

Is **this** Bank of India?
Yes. It is. You can open an account at **this** bank if you want to.
This is the cash counter. **These** are the paying-in counters.
That's the foreign exchange counter. What for?
You can buy and sell foreign money here.
This is the bank manager's room. **Those** are toilets.
That's inquiries over there.

▪ One/Ones

'One' can be used in place of a noun; 'ones' is the plural of 'one'.
These are commonly used in selection and comparison.

Look at the examples :

- This **coat** : this **one**; these **coats** : these **ones**.
- Buy this **coat**. Buy this **one**.
- No, this **one** is ordinary. Then, buy that **one**.
- Which are expensive, these **ones** or those **ones**?

(of) people :

Say : These boys are very intelligent.
This **one** is genius at maths and the **one** in the white shirt is an expert singer.
Look at those tall **ones** standing over there. They're very good at basketball.

▪ (a) 'This' and 'that' can introduce people

Say : This is .... (When introducing someone), eg :

- This is my wife, Joyti. This is Amit from Delhi.
- That's Mr Sinha. He's my next-door neighbour.

(b) This/that can be used for time references, eg.

He was here this day (= today).

Also : this morning/this afternoon/this evening, eg.

- He came **this** morning. (= In the morning today)
- **This** winter is the coldest since 1990. (This : of this year)
- Deepawali festival ends **this** Tuesday. (= Coming Tuesday)
- He's flying to Mumbai **this** evening. (= In the evening today)

Say : that day/**that** night/**that** morning/**that** time, eg :

- It rained heavily **that** day. I was a schoolboy at **that** time. (= Then)
- **These** days people are more conscious of their rights. (= Nowadays)
- In **those** days there was no electricity. (= During that time)

(c) This/that : used when making phone calls

Look at the examples :

Hello! Is **that** 2458756?
Is **that** you, Pinki? **This** is Sonia here.
Hello, **this** is Sangeeta.
Can I speak to Mr. Raj, Please?
Receptionist : Taj Hotel.
Good morning! Can I help you?
Kishan : This is Kishan speaking.
Could I speak to Dr. Bhagav please?

(d) Consider the following expressions :

This way; this and that; that is; this is how
What's all this? That's why

Look at the examples:

Please take him to the Principal's office .... Come this way, sir.
This and that : All sorts of things, eg :
He went on talking about this end that.
What's all this? (What's going on?/What's the matter here?)
That is : used 'to clarify' something, eg;
Our exams start on the 15th, **that is**, on Tuesday.
That's why : for this reason, eg.
They got stuck in a traffic jam; that's why they arrived late.
This is how : in this way
He hid himself behind a tree; this is how he could save himself.

Unit-21 Identifying People
(लोगों की पहचान)

Who ....? (used to identify people)

When I say, "Who are you" I am asking you to disclose your identity. 'identity' can be disclosed in several ways the commonest of which is to tell your name. The answer to the above question can be :

- **I'm** Anil, etc. (Give your name)
  (Or) I'm Mr Sharma's son.
  I'm your next-door neighbour, etc.

  Look at the following examples : (On the phone) :
  - Hello! Who's speaking, please? (= Please tell me your name)
  - **Who's** crying at this hour of night!/**Who** rang you this morning?
  - **Who** broke the windowpane?/Hello, I'm Monika. Who are you?

Whoever : any person who

"Whoever" can be used as **subject** or **object** in a sentence.
As the **subject**, it asks **emphatic** question, **eg;**
- **Whoever** is responsible for this crime shall be punished.
- **Whoever** told you that, I think is a liar.
- **Whoever** phones, tell them I'm out.

As object it means : 'anybody or the person who', eg.
- Give this money to **whoever** you please.
- **Whoever** you marry, make sure she can cook, etc.

- **When pointing to someone at a distance**
  (जब दूर से किसी की ओर इशारा करते हैं)

  Don't say : Who is he? Who is she?
  Who's **that** woman over there? The answer can be :
  That's our new English teacher. Would you like to meet him?
  That/It's my neighbour's wife, Gauri.
  Note : 'It' can also be used to identify people.

- **Identifying people** (लोगों की पहचान) (= to know who the person is)

(a) Say : Who is it?/Who is there? (**Not :** Who is he/she?)

(b) If somebody's knocking at the door (यदि कोई दरवाजा खटखटा रहा हो)

Say : Who is it? (= Kaun hai?)

Response : **It's** the postman/It's **me**, Amit.
It's Monika, your neighbour, etc.

(c) There's somebody in the garden :

Say : Who is **it**?
Response : I think it's your uncle.

(d) There's somebody behind the curtain :

Say : Who is **it**?
Oh, it's you! (You already know him well)

(e) Look at that man smoking a cigar!

Who is it?
Response : I don't know, Perhaps it's Peter.

(f) Who phoned you last night?

Response : It was Amit.

- **A request for details** (विवरण के लिए अनुरोध)

Example :

Q. : Who is **she**?
Ans : She's my **friend**. She lives next door.
Q. : Who's **he**?
Ans : He's my **boss**. He's from South India.
Q. : Who's Mr **Sharma**?
Ans : He's captain in the army.
Q. : Who's Monika?
Ans : She's my **friend**. We're classmates.
Q. : Who's Mrs. Bhatia?
Ans : She's my **friend's aunt**.
Q. : Who are they?
Ans : They're my **tenants**.

Whom? (Object form of 'who')

Note : "Whom" is rarely used now; people prefer "who" instead. it serves for both **subject** and **object** in the sentence.

Don't say : Whom do you want to meet? (Formal)

Say : Who do you want to meet? (Spoken form)

Look at the following examples :

Ans : He met the **Secretary**.
Q. : Who did he meet? (**Don't say :** Whom did he meet?)
Ans : The boy helped the **Old man**.
Q. : **Who** did the boy help?
Ans : She's marrying her **boyfriend**.
Q. : **Who's** she marrying?
Ans : He invited his **teacher**.
Q. : **Who** did he invite?

- **Who (m)?**

Use who/that (or avoid both)

Look at these examples :

Don't say : The woman whom I met yesterday is an actress.

Say : The woman who I met yesterday is an actress.

- The woman **that** I met yesterday is an actress.
- The woman I met yesterday is an actress. (Avoid 'that')

- **Put the preposition at the end of the sentence**

Don't say : To whom were you talking? (Formal)

Say : Who were you talking **to**? (Spoken form)

The man to whom I complained is a police officer. (Formal)

The man who/that I complained **to** is a police officer.

Look at the examples:	**(Short question)**
1. (She was writing to her mother)	
Who was she writing **to**?	**Who to**?
2. (He was staring at her)	
Who was he staring **at**?	**Who at**?
3. (She was dancing with her friend)	
Who was she dancing with?	**Who with**?
4. (He bought it for his mother)	
Who did he buy it **for**?	**Who for**?
5. (I got this letter from him)	
Who did you get this letter **from**?	**Who from**?

Whose? (used to identify the possessor)

The 'Possessor' (स्वामी) is a person who possesses or owns something.

Look at the examples :

- **Whose** book is this? **Whose** books are these?
- **Whose** pens is this? **Whose** pens are those?

▪ The following words answer the question "Whose?"

Adjectives : my, your, his, her, our, their, its, ones

Pronouns : mine, yours, his, hers, ours, theirs

Look at the examples : (questions and answers)

Q. : **Whose** house is this?
Ans : This is **my** house. This house is **mine**. It's **mine**.
Q. : **Whose** house is **that**?
Ans : That's my house. It's **mine**.
Q. : **Whose** books are these?
Ans : Are these **yours**, Priyanka? yes, they're **mine**.
Q. : **Whose** bicycle is that? it's Pinki's.
Ans : That's her bicycle. It's **hers**.
Q. : **Whose** coat is this?
Ans : It's my **brother's** coat. It's **his** coat. Yes, it's **his**.
Q. : **Whose** umbrellas are these? Those're the girls.
Ans : These're **theirs** not **ours**.

▪ Look at the following examples :

- The man **whose** car broke down is my colleague.
- A woman **whose** husband is dead is called window.
- The actress **whose** film we saw is a singer as well.
- Mr Dass **whose** factory we work in is a kind man.
- David **whose** courage saved us is a brave officer.

▪ Possessive pronouns may come at the beginning

Look at the examples:

- **Mine** is a red coat; **yours** is blue. **His** is a muscular body.
- **Hers** is a beautiful face. **Theirs** is a rich country; **ours** is poor.
- Is your father a doctor? **Mine** is an engineer.
- Their principal is very strict; **ours** is very kind.

- **Look at these sentences :**

Whose chair is this? (Or) **Whose** is this?

This is **my** chair/this is **mine**.

Whose books are these? (Or) **Whose** are these?

These are **mine**, not **yours**.

Whose house is No. 10? **Whose** is No. 10?

Pooja's house is No. 10.

Whose shoes are these? **Whose** are these?

They're Mannu's.

- **Don't omit the noun after "Whose" if it is a person.**

Look at the example :

Don't say : Whose are you? Say : Whose **son/daughter** are you?

Look at the examples :

Whose **son** are you?	Mr Rakesh's (= I'm Mr Sunil Kumar's son)
Whose **brother** are you?	Sony's (= I'm Sony's brother)
Whose daughters are you?	**Mrs Anita's** (= Mrs Anita's daughters)
Whose **Children** are they?	The Sharma' (= The Sharmas' children)
Whose wife is Sunita?	**Mr Modi's** (Mr Modi's wife)

- **Put the preposition at the end of the sentence**

Look at the examples :

For **whose** benefit has the government introduced this bill? (Formal)

Whose benefit has the government introduced this **bill** for? (Informal)

He's the man **from whose** gun the shot was fired. (Formal)

He's the man **whose** gun the shot was fired from? (informal)

This is the man **from whose** shop the jewellery was stolen. (Formal)

This is the man **whose** shop, the jewellery was stolen **from**?

- **Consider these sentences :**

Whose side are you **on**? (Spoken from)

He's buying a car next week : **With** whose money?

(**Not** "whose money with?")

He finally succeeded in his plan? With whose help did he...?

(**Not** "Whose help with?")

❑❑❑

Unit-22 Identifying People and Things

(व्यक्ति और वस्तुओं की पहचान करना)

What?/Which?

'What' and 'which' as question-words are used to identify people and things. They have the same form for singular and plural. "What" asks general questions whereas "Which" inquires about specific ones.

- **What ....? (Of things)**

Look at the examples :

What trees grow in India?/**what** opens this door?/**what** film is on at the Plaza?

What book are you reading?/**what** lipstick do you use?/**what** books did you buy?

What Paper do you read?/ **what** subjects are you taking at university?

What delayed you?

What ....? (Of people)

What people live in this village? **What people** did you meet at the party?

What men are fit for mountaineering? / **What boy(s)** are you talking about?

Note : the use of 'who(m)' is preferable to 'what' in these sentence.

- **What ...? (Of things and animals)**

Look at the examples :

What's this?	it's my brush/coffee/dog.
What's that?	That's a chair / tree/bird/camel.
What are these/those?	These/those are sheep and goats.

What is it? It's a button/five-rupee note/an insect, etc.

Compare : Who is it?

- **Put the preposition at the end of the sentence**

Look at the examples :

- What did he open the door **with**?/What's that machine **for**?
- What's this chair made **of**? / What are you looking **for**?

- What did she did **of**?/ What fool are you talking **about**?
- What's this money for?

Note : die of = be the cause of death, eg :
Die of fever/exposure/cancer/pneumonia/starvation, etc.

That/Which

'That' and 'which' are used as joining words for things and animals. 'That' is more common; 'which' is rather formal.

Look at the examples :

- The plane **that/which** was flying low crashed to the ground.
- The film that/which is attracting crowds is full of violence.
- Buffaloes **that/which** go dry are sent to slaughterhouse.

In everyday speech joining words can be dropped, eg.

1. Look at this digital watch that/which I bought yesterday.
   Look at this digital watch I bought yesterday. (spoken form)
2. These are the 3-G phones that/which I bought from Delhi.
   These are the 3-G phones I bought from Delhi.

Learn the uses of in/on/where/when :

1. The office **in which** my brother works is opposite the station.
   The office my brother **works in** is opposite the station. (Preferable)
   The office **where** my brother works is opposite the station. (Preferable)
2. Sunday is the day **on which** most people stay at home.
   Sunday is the day **when** most people stay at home. (Pfeferable)
3. The months **during which** I was in London are unforgettable.
   The months **when** I was in London are unforgettable. (Pfeferable)
4. The college in **which I** studied is a centre of higher education.
   The college **where** I studied is a centre of higher education. (Pfeferable)
5. It was the year of serious drought **in which** my eldest son was born.
   It was the year of serious drought when my eldest son was born.

■ The difference between its and it's

Don't confuse its (possessive) with it's = it is.

Remember :

"Its" is used to show that something belongs to a thing/place/animal etc.

"Whose" can replace 'its'

Look at the following examples :

- This is my cup. **Its** handle is broken. (its = of the cup)
- The cup **Whose** handle is broken is mine.
- This blazer is mine. **Its** pockets are torn.
- The blazer **whose** pockets are torn is mine.

'Of which'

'Of which' indicates possession; it can replace 'whose.'

Look at the examples:

- The cup **whose** handle is broken is mine.
- The cup **of which** the handle is broken is mine.
- The house **whose** windows are broken belongs to my uncle.
- The house **of which** the windows are broken belongs to my uncle.
- The vehicle **whose** brakes are loose might cause an accident.
- The vehicle of **which** the brakes are loose might cause an accident.
- He has made a film **whose** songs are a big hit.
- he has made a film the songs **of which** are a big hit.

'Of which'

This is used in formal situations, eg.

- The chairman had a meeting the purpose of **which** was to promote export.
- He filed an affidavit the content **of which** could not be immediately known.
- It was a secret pact the details **of which** were not made public.

'Prepositional phrases' are a better choice than 'of which'

Look at the examples :

- The house **of which** the windows are broken belongs to my uncle.
- The old house with the broken windiows belongs to my uncle.
- The diary **of which** the pages are torn belongs to Mr John.
- The diary with the torn pages belongs to Mr John.

"Whose" can be used for plants, animals, etc.

Look at the examples :

- The cow whose milk is very useful should be taken good care of.
- The cobra **whose** poison is deadly is the most feared creature.
- My uncle's dog, **whose** ears are long, often attacks passerby.
- Thees **whose** leaves drop in the autumn appear again in the spring.

Unit-23 Describing Appearance
(उपस्थिति वर्णन)

'Appearance' refers to someone's looks, shape and size. it also means, features like hair, eyes, nose, mouth etc. In this unit we are going to discuss about 'hair' and 'complexion'. Other physical features will be deait with at length in the next unit. To begin with, let's talk about 'complexion' first.

Complexion (रंग-ढंग, रंगरूप, स्वभाव)

Complexion is the natural colour of a person's skin that adds attractiveness to his or her physical appearance. It can be : **fair, dark** or **whitish** (note the spelling). Fair is light in colour, whitish is pale and almost white; dark is nearer black than light.

Look at the examples:

What colour is his/her skin?

Meaning : What kind of skin colour has he/she got?

Answer :

She is/She's **fair**. She has/she's got a **whitish** complexion.

She's **fair** complexioned/he's **dark**.

(or) he's **dark-complexioned**, etc.

- **Describing hair** (बालों का वर्णन करना)

Don't say 'hairs'

Say 'hair' if you mean **all the hair** on a person's head.

Look at the examples :

Incorrect	Correct
She has long **hairs**.	She has long **hair**.
His hairs are **grey**.	His hair is **grey**.
He was combing his **hairs**.	He was combing his **hair**.

Remember : 'Hair' is an **uncountable** noun. If you are referring to '**all the hair**' on someone's head, the verb should be singular. 'Hair' is **countable** if you are talking about '**a single**' or several '**individual hair**' the verb can be **singular** or **Plural** as the case may be.

Look at the following examples :

- Her hair is black/don't let your **hair** down.
- He cut the few white **hairs** off his head.
- There's **a** long black **hair** in your soup.
- Let me brush **the hairs** off your shirt.
- He had **a few** sparse **hairs** on his chin.

■ Your hair can be (आपके बाल हो सकते हैं)

Black/white/grey/dark/brown/red/blond

Black is the **darkest colour**; **white** is the lightest colour; **grey** is between black and white **Dark** is nearer black; **brown** is the colour of coffee or toasted beard and **blond** is yellowish (= golden)

■ Describing hair (बालों का वर्णन)

Look at the examples :

Q. : What colour is Mona's hair?
Ans : It's grey.
Q. : What colour is his moustache?
Ans : It is/it's white. It's black.

Note : In spoken English, it is more common to say.

I've got/you've got ..., etc. than saying : I have/you have ....

Say : What colour of that girls's hair?

Answer : She has/she's got blond hair. (=She has blond hair)
Her hair's (= hair is) a nice dark colour/she's got dark lovely hair.
She's (= she has) got dark hair. (Or) she's dark-haired.

Complimenting someone's hair (किसी के बालों की तारीफ करना)

Say : What beautiful black hair you've got!

■ Say : What's her hair like? (What kind of hair has she got?)

Look at these examples :

She has/she's got **short** hari. (She is short-haired)

Q. : What's her mother's hair like (to look at)?
Ans : She's got **long** hair. (She's long-haired)
Kavita's got **wavy** shoulder-length hair. (Wavy = growing in waves)
Look at the woman with **golden** ringlets? (Long loose curls of hair)
Q. : What's her hair like?
Ans : She's got long **golden** ringlets.
Q. : Who came today?
Ans : A **clean-shaven** gentleman came this morning.

Q. : What was he like (to look at)?
Ans : He was quite old with greying **curly** hair.
Q. : Who came with him?
Ans : It was a middle-aged man with **straight** hair.
Q. : What's your father's hair like?
Ans : It's **thinning** on top (= He's getting bald)
Q. : What are his eyebrows like?
Ans : He's got **thick bushy** eyebrows.
(Bushy = growing thickly)
Q. : What was that Sadhu's hair like?
Ans : He'd got matted hair. (He'd = he had)

Fairly/quite/rather

The adverbs given above answer the question : **"to what extent?"** When someone says : her hair is **'fairly grey'** means : "to some extent", not **"too grey"**. **'Quite'** means the same, eg; her hair's **quite grey**. **'Rather'** suggests almost the same idea, but at times it conveys more than this, that is : **"too much"**, eg : Her hair's **rather** grey.

Go/get/turn = become.

Look at the examples

Your hair's (= hair has) **gone** white/you're **getting** bald.

She used to have dark hair, but now it's (= it has) **turned** grey (almost white)

- **Describing someone's moustaches/beards** (लोगों के दाढ़ी और मूछों का वर्णन)

Look at these adjectives :

Long, short, trimmed, flowing white, grey

Examples (questions and answers) :

Q. : What's his beard like? (= What sort of beard has he?)
Ans : It's long and **grey**.
Q. : What about his moustache?
Ans : He's got short moustache.
Q. : Who's (who is) that man with a **neatly trimmed** bread?
Ans : He's my immediate boss.
Q. : What was the old man's beard like (to look at)?
Ans : It was a **white flowing** beard.

Wear : Have/use

People **were** 'hairstyle' to give a stylish look to their hair.
Look at the examples :
Radha wears her hair in a ponytail.
She likes **wearing** her hair in a fashionable style/ I **wear** my hair long.
Which hairstyle do you **wear**? he was **wearing** a French cut beard.

Here are some more examples :

She **wore** a black wig over her white **hair**.
Some women wear garlands of white roses round their buns.
People now a days **wear** hairstyles of their favourite stars.
Young people **wear** long curly hair/he was **wearing** a beard.
She **wears** a hair band/ribbon in her hair. I **wear** a hairnet over my hair.

- **Look at these examples :**

Why don't you wear a hairnet? It'll keep your hair tidy (= neatly arranged)
Your hair's a **mess! Comb** it before you go to school. (Mess = in disorder)
Tie up your hair **at the back** with a **hair band**.
She plucked a flower and **inserted** it **into** her hair.
Brush **your** hair/he gave his hair a **quick brush** and went out.
Oil your hair after you have taken a bath. (Oil = rub oil on your hair)
What do you do after **oiling** your hair?/ **Dye** your hair; it's (it has) **turned** grey.

Hair style (बालों के बनावट/प्रकार/अंदाज)

Women wear different types of hairstyle, eg : Ponytail/plaiting/bun/bob, etc.
In the **ponytail** hairstyle hair is tied in a bunch at the back of the head hanging down like a norse's taill.
In the **plait/braid** style, one or two long pieces of hair are twisted/plaited and tied together to make one long piece.

Look at the example :

- Anita **plaited** har hair hurriedly and went out/she wears her hair in **plaits**.
- In **Bun** hairstyle, hair is gathered into a tight round shapes as the back of the head.

Example : My mother wears her hair in a bun.
Bob is a hairstyle in which the hair is cut short at the front and all round the head, eg.

She wants to have (= got) her hair **bobbed**/Madhu got her hair bobbed (=cut)/ the smart lady with a **bob** is a model/she wears her hair in a **bob**.

- **Combing hair (बालों में कंघा करना)**

Look at the example :

He has dark **curly** hair combed **to the left** (to the left side)

(a) The parting : the 'line' separating hair on the head, eg.

Most people like a **side parting** (to the left or to its right)

He has a **side parting**.

(b) Centre parting : It refers to the line a person makes with a comb in the centre of his/her head, eg.

The woman with vermilion (sindoor) in the **centre parting** is my aunt.

Women usually comb their hair with a **centre parting**.

- **Shaving hair (बालों का हजामत)**

learn the folloing words and expressions :

(a) Shave : (v) cutting hair from the face or a part of the body (with a razor/knife) eg.

He's **shaving**/the barber **shaved** his head/I washed and **shaved** before going out/she **shaves** her legs and under her arms.

Shave off : to cut off (remove) hair from the face, eg.

he **shaved off** his moustache and the beard.

(b) Shave : (noun) (**सेव/हजामत बनाना**)

Look at these examples :

You **need a shave**. Go to the barber's (shop) / Did you **have a shave** this morning?/ The barber **gave** him a **close shave**/Do you want to **have a wet shave?/**You can't **have a good** shave with a cheap razor.

(c) Learn the following words and expressions :

Shaven : (adj.) with all the hair shaved off, eg.

I saw the old gentleman with his **shaven** head.

Clean-shaven : (adj.) with the face hair **shaved off,**

Examples : Do you know that **clean-shaven** man?

It's good to be **clean-shaven** and smart.

- **Going to the barber's (shop) (नाई के पास जाना) (दुकान)**

Barber is a person whose job is shaving and haircutting.

A **hairdresser** not only cuts hair but also gives a style to your hair.

Look at the exampels :

- I'm going for **a haircut**. Where do you **get** your **hair cut** from?
- I **get** my **hair cut** at the **barber's** (shop)

Note : 'shop' is not used at the end in everyday speech.

Q. : When did you last **get** your **haircut?**

Ans : I last **got** my **hair cut** a month ago.

Q. : **Who** (= whom) did you **get** your **hair cut** from?
Why don't you get your **hair cut?** It's too long.

Ans : I'm going to **get** my **haircut** just now.

Note : 'have' can be used instead of 'get'.

Unit-24 Describing Appearance

(उपस्थिति वर्णन)

- **Facial features (चेहरे की विशेषताएँ)**

Face is the outside shape of a person's appearance; eyes, ears, nose, mouth and cheeks are its physical features. A person with attractive features is considered be more attractive than a person with an ordinary face.

Face-wise people have either round or ovar face; 'Oval' means : egg-shapped.

'-faced' when combines with words, such as red, round, thin, indicates shape.

Look at the examples :

Her face is **round** (= She's round-faced)

her face is **round** (= she's ovar-faced)

- **Describing eyes : (आँखों का वर्णन)**

People have different types of eyes : big, small, dark, beautiful, etc.

Squint (n/v) :

Squint is an eye disorder. A person suffering from this defect looks in different directions when he turns his eyes together. Such a person is called **squint-eyed**.

Look at the examples :

He has a squint. (= he's squint-eyed)/he squinted at the brightly coloured objects/she squinted in the dazzling light/he squinted as he took aim at the target.

- **One-eyed (काना) :** a one-eyed person has only one eye.

Look at the examples :

He's a one-eyed man/the man who wears glasses is one-eyed.

Blind (अंधा) : a person who is unable to see, eg; He's blind/he's blind in the left eye.

- **A person's eyes can be :** hollow, bulging or sunken.

Hollow (खाली, खोखला) : eyes that have empty space inside are called hollow, eg.

He has hollow eyes/he started at me with his hollow eyes.

Bulging (उभरा हुआ) : Bulging eyes look as if coming out from their sockets, eg.
His bulging eyes frightened me/his face is round and eyes bulging.

Sunken (धँसा हुआ) : Someone's eyes that have gone inwards are called sunken eyes, eg;
His sunken eyes flashed wheh I put a hundred-rupee note on his palm.

- **Lips/ears/nose/cheeks (ओंठ, कान, नाक, गाल) :**

Lips (ओंठ) : You have two lips - the lower and the upper lip.

Lips can be : dry, thick or twisted, eg. she has thick lips. (= She's thick-lipped)
Her lips are dry/his lips are twisted, etc.

- **Ears (कान) :** people have-Long/short/big/small ears.

A person with long ears is calld long-eared, eg.
He's long-eared/he's short-eared

Left ear/right ear :

'Left' and 'right' indicate position of an ear on the head, eg.
Which ear do you have a pain in? I often have a sharp pain in my left ear, etc.

- **Nose (नाक) :** the shape and size of a person's nose has great importance.

Its pleasing symmetry adds to the sharpness of one's features.

Someone's nose can be long/flat/pointed/red etc.

Look at the examples :

His nose is flat/he's flat-nosed/he's got a flat nosed with wide nostrils.
His nose is long and pointed/the red-nosed girl is my classmate, etc.

- **Cheeks (गाल) :** The following words can be used to describe someone's cheeck :

Rosy, chubby, plump, bulging, swollen, hollow

Examples :

- The girl has a beauty spot on her rosy cheeks.
- Chubby, plump and bulging cheeks are fat and round.
- Swollen cheeks are large in size.
- Hollow indicates empty space inside, eg.
- He's hollow-cheeked, etc.

- **Making a request for describing someone, eg :**

"What does he like?" (= describe his physical appearance)

Answer : He's dark, tall and a little overweight.

What's Saniya like (as a person)?

She's slim, tall and very beautiful.

What's her nose like (to look at)?

It's long and pointed, etc.

- **What's .... like/**

This question can also be used to describe someone's character.

Besides, it can describe one's ability or skill (to do something), eg :

What's he/she like?

Response : He's honest/intelligent/dull, etc.
He's genius at physics.

She's clever/good/very good **at** knitting .... etc. In the same way :

He's excellent/first rate/good/quite good/bad/not bad **at** .....

- **What's he like? What's she like?**

The following adjectives can be used to answer the above questions :

- **Pretty :** pleasant to look at (used esp. of a woman or child), **eg.**
  - She's a pretty girl/she looks much prettier with her bob hair.
  - She's an attractive girl/he's an attractive young man
- **Charming :** Very pleasing or attractive (used of men and women), eg.
  - She's a charming girl.
  - He's a man of charming personality (a source of inspiration)
- **Beautiful :** extremely good to look at; very pleasing (used of women), eg.
  - She's beatutiful.
  - she has a beautiful face, etc.
- **Handsome :** (esp. of a man) physically attractive; good looking, eg.
  - He's very handsome/he's handsome fellow.

  Note : 'handsome' can also be used to describe a woman provided :
  She is strong looking, attractive with a large appearance.
  Such women often lack feminine delicacies.
- **Good-looking :** a person with an attractive face (used of men and women), eg.
  - They both are good-looking.
  - She's tall and good-looking.
  - What a good-looking man he is!

- **Smart :** neat and clean; well dressed, eg.
  - He's extremely smart and neatly dressed.
  - He/she's looking smart in his/her grey suit.
- **Elegant :** beautiful/ graceful/ stylish, eg. She's a tall, elegant woman/ he's an elegant person, etc.

■ Talking about shape and size (आकृति और आकार के बारे में बातचीत)

Look at these words : **big, small, little**

'Big' is used for grown up children who are now large in size.

Look at the examples :

- Don't cry; you're a big child now.
- I was quite big when I started going to school.
- You can't compete with the big boys of your class, said her mother.
- The teacher made the big boy monitor of the class.

Small : Less than average in size, eg.

- He's small man, only five feet tall.
- She has three small children.
- He's small for his age.

Little : not big, eg.

- She was carrying her little girl.
- The little boy was begging in the street.
- You're too little to ride a bicycle.
- The little old lady is my English teacher.

■ **Build :** a person's build is the shape of his/her body.

People with fleshy body are called :

Fat obese heavy overweight bulky

Overweight : people who are overweight are **too fat** (= obese)

Note : It is not polite to call someone fat, better say :

He's overweight/ a little overweight, etc.

■ Consider the following words :

- **Plump (मोटा) :** a person with a soft rounded body (slightly fat), eg : A plump woman.

  Examples :
  - You're getting a bit plump'.
  - you're too plump to wear these jeans.
  - The plump lady is famous fashion designer, etc.

- **Chubby (गोल-मटोल) :** fat and rounded (in a pleasant and attractive way) This word is often used to describe children and young adults, eg :
  - Chubby cheeks.
  - I like her chubby smilling face.

- **These words show a person in his normal health**
(ये शब्द व्यक्ति के सामान्य स्वास्थ्य को दर्शाता है)
Slim Slender Lean Thin
  - **Slim (छरहरा, दुबला-पतला) :** a person who has reduced his/her body weight by dieting and taking exercise, ***e.g.*** :
    - He exercises every morning to get slim.
    - She's on a diet. She's slimming.
  - **Slender (दुबला, पतला, सुडौल) :** thin and graceful, *e.g.;*
    - She's slender.
    - She has a slender figure.
  - **Lean (दुबला) :** slim (a person without much fat) *e.g.*
    - He's a lean and handsome fellow.
    - Lean girls with attractive face are beautiful.
  - **Thin (दुबला, पतला) :** person with no extra fat on his/her body, *e.g.*
    - She's short and thin.
    - He has become very thin after his illness.

Note : 'slim' indicates good health; 'thin' suggests little flesh on the bones.

- **Words that can describe different parts of your body :**
High/ wide/ broad/ round/ flat/ tender/ slender/ flabby
Look at the examples :
  - He has a high (= wide) forehead.
  - He is /he's broad shoulder (= he has shoulders that are bent forward)
  - She's tender/ slender waisted (= having a gracefully thin waist)
  - She's rather flat chested (= having small breasts)

Flabby : someone with soft/loose flesh and muscle, *e.g.*
  - The man with his long flabby face is the owner of this car.
  - Her arms, legs and buttocks are getting flabby (loose).

- **Look like =** appears to be (used to describe appearance), *e.g.*
He looks like (= is similar) to his father when he smiles.
What does he look like? (वह कैसा दिखता है?)
(A request for general information about someone's appearance)

Examples : (questions and answer)

Q. : What does Monika look like? She's tall, fair with average looks.

Ans : She's got dark curly hair.

Q. : What does Shruti look like?

Ans : She's 5.6″ tall,, fair, beautiful and slim.
She's got big eyes and her hair's a nice dark colour.
She's got a beauty spot on one of her rosy cheeks.

Q. : What does he look like?

Ans : He' short and dark complexioned.
He'e got round shoulders and a trimmed beard.
His buttocks are heavy, cheeks fat and rounded.

A : **Have you seen the killer?**

Ans : Yes. He's dark; short and thin and has bulging eyes.

B : **What does he look like?**

Ans : He's got a flat nose with wide nostrils.

- **Questions on similarity in appearance** (दिखने में समानता पर प्रश्न)

Don't say : "Whom....?"

Say : "Who ...?"

Look at the examples :

Q. : Who does Amit look like?

Ans : Amit looks like his father.

Q. : Who does Sonia look like.

Ans : Sonia looks like her mother.

Q. : Who does she look like?

Ans : She looks like Malvika.

Q. : Who does Poonam's face look like?

Ans : Poonam's face looks like her mother's.

Q. : Who does her hair look like?

Ans : Her hair looks like her sister's.

- **The following phrases express the same idea :**

Look like/ look alike/ exactly like/just like

Exmaples :

Who(m) does Amit look like? He looks like his father.
Amit and his father look alike. (= Amit is exactly like his father)
They're just alike.

❑❑❑

Unit-25 Talking about education (I)
(शिक्षा के बारे में बातचीत)

Stages in education (शिक्षा के चरण)

Education in India is organized in three stages : the first one includes primary education, the second consists of secondary education and the third stage is of university education. After passing exams at primary school, the child enters a secondary school that finally leads him into a college or university.

- **School education (स्कूली शिक्षा) :** types of student

  Children at primary school are **pupils** or **kids**; at secondary school they are called schoolboys or schoolgirls. If a student **leaves** school without completing the course, he is known as a **dropout**. Someone who has **left** school for a job is called a **school leaver**.

- **Admission/Admit to (प्रवेश/दाखिला)**

  A child is admitted **to** a class after considering his previous record. He is **re-tested** if the original results do not seem accurate; in case he is found suitable he is given admission. The class teacher writes his name **into** the register after charging **tution fee**. If the fee is not paid regularly his name is **struck off** the **roll** (= the register).

- **School time (विद्यालय का समय)**

  Q. : What time does your school start/finish?

  Ans : It starts **at** 10:00 in the morning and finishes **at** 3:30.

- **School bell (विद्यालय की घंटी)**

  The bell goes/rings : makes a sound

  Examples :

  - The school bell is ringing; let's hurry up.
  - When the bell **rings**, children assemble for prayer.
  - Children rush home when the bell **goes** at 3:30.
  - Get ready; the bell will **ring** in a minute or two.
  - The bell **has gone**. Let's go home, now.

- **On the roll (British English)**

  Roll : a roll is a list of **names** (= register), *e.g.*

- There's a school quite near with 500 students on the roll.
- There are more than 30 students on the roll in this class.

Take/call the roll (v) = take attendance (Am Eng)

The teacher reads aloud the names **on the roll** to make sure that all the pupils are present in the class. **Absentees** are marked 'A'.

Look at the examples :

The teacher was **calling the roll** (= taking attendance)

He **took attendance** (= called the roll) after the break.

Roll call (n) : calling of names from the attendance register, *e.g.*

- The teacher took the **roll call** (= took attendance)
- He **slipped out** after the roll call/See me after the roll call.
- The teacher took the roll call to see if any students were absent.

▪ High/low/poor/thin attendance

Look at the examples :

- Attendance **at** evening classes is very high/low.
- Attendance **at** school was very poor this morning.
- The attendance **at** the prayer was rather thin.

▪ Learn these words : skip/miss, eg :

If you **skip** classes, you'll do badly in the exam.

He sometimes **skips** English class, doesn't he?

Skip (v) = to fail to attend/miss.

▪ Break time (अवकाश)

Break/recess : a short period of time **for** rest **at** school, eg :

- Children **have** (= take) lunch **at** break. They often meet during recess.
- Children go outdoors and play **in** the recess/break. (Outdoors = outside)
- When's break time **at** your school?/you can meet her at break.

▪ To/from

Talking about kids :

Q. : Who **takes** you **to** school?

Ans : My dad (takes me to school)

Q. : Who comes **to take** you **from** school?

Ans : (My Mom (not dad)

My mother comes **to collect** me **from** school.

Q. : Who **picks** you **up** from school? (= Brings you back)

Ans : My Mother comes **to pick** me **up** from school.

Q. : Who **brings** you **back** from school?

Ans : My Mother **brings** me **back** from school.

Talking about big (= older) boys and girls

Q. : How do you go to school?

I go **on foot** (=by walking).

I **walk to** school every day. My sister runs to school.

The school is **a ten minutes' walk** from here.

Q. : Can **I walk it** (= walk the distance)?

Ans : Why not? You can **walk down** the space easily. (= walk along)

Q. : How do you **get back** home?

Ans : **I stroll** all along the way home.

Stroll : to walk slowly (without hurrying).

Q. : Can you **ride** a bicycle? (= sit on a bike and move along)

Ans : Yes, **I ride** to school every morning. (= go sitting on a bike)

At times my mother **drives** me to school. (= takes me to school in the car)

When my scooter is punctured, **I ride** with my friend **on** his bicycle.

Lots of my friends **ride on** your scooter? By all means! (= Certainly)

- **Schoolmate** = your school friend
  - My father met an old schoolmate from Delhi.
  - They were schoolmates forty years ago.

- **Does your school organize pleasure trips?**

  Learn the following words and their uses :

  - **Trip : a short journey for pleasure, eg.**
  - Is your son **going on** the school trip **to** Kashmir?
  - Our school is **organizing** a boat trip **down** the river Ganges.
  - Our class is **taking/making** a trip **to** the mountains.
  - **Tour : a journey for pleasure, eg.**
  - Our class teacher **took** us **on** a sightseeing tour of the city.
  - **Sightseeing : visiting famous/interesting place, eg.**
  - We'll go sightseeing/we **went** sightseeing in Delhi.
  - They'll **take** us **on** a tour **round/around** the city of Taj.
  - We **toured** the hottest area of Rajasthan last week.
  - We're **going on** a 15-day tour of Singapore.

- Have they **come back from** the tour?

◆ **Outing/excursion (भ्रमण/सैर) : a trip to a place of interest, *e.g.***

- They're **going on** a class/school outing **to** Tajmahal.
- We're **going on** an excursion next week.

◆ **Excursion** = a short journey/trip

◆ **Picnic :** an occasion when children are taken out on small trips.

Examples :

- Our class is **going on/for** a picnic on sunday.
- We **went on/for** a picnic yesterday.

❑❑❑

Unit-26 Talking about education (II)

(शिक्षा के बारे में बातचीत)

Omission of 'the' With School

Don't Say : I'm going to the school.

Say : I'm going to **school**.

Remember : 'the' **with** school is not used if the purpose of visit is to **attend classes;** if the visit is for some other purpose, the use of 'the' is correct. **Likewise :** Don't use 'the' with **'class/classes'** if the purpose is **studying,** eg. She's in class (= studying); in other situations its use is correct. The same rule applies to college or university.

Look at the following examples :

Amit is in **class** (= studying)/ she rarely attends **classes**.
Teaching would be more effective if **classes** were smaller.
Classes have been cancelled because of heavy rain.
You'll be late for **school/classes** if you don't hurry up.
No talking in **class**. Stop making a noise in **class**.

- **Don't Say :** in the school.
  Say : in **school** (=studying)

  Look at the examples :

  You must obey your teachers in school.
  She was in **school** when I got the message.
  Children were in **School** when the fire broke out.
  We were detained in **school** for extra classes.

- **Use 'the' if the purpose of visit is other than studying**

  Look at the examples :

  - Excuse me, where's **the** school? (= The school building)
  - Mother has gone to **the** school to talk to my teacher. (Not to study)
  - There's a parent-teacher meeting at **the** school this afternoon.
  - He's at **the** school now. (He has arrived at the school)
  - They are in **the** school. (= In the school building)

- **Have/take/give lesson = learn/teach something, *e.g.***
  - I'm **having/taking** lessons in English these days.

- He's a marvelous actor. Has he **taken** acting lessons?
- She **gives** lessons in French. (= She teaches French)
- I didn't enter the class because they were having a lesson.
- The retired professor is having/taking lessons in music.
- Mr Raman **takes** (= teaches) maths at school.

Take a test/an exam

Examples:

- You have to **take** a qualifying test **for** admission **to** this course.
- Children have to **take** the exam **for** admission **to** the nursery class.
- I'm **taking** my mid-term exams next week.

■ **Sit for :** take an exam, *e.g.*

- She's **sitting for** pre-school test this year.
- He **sat for** the scholarship exam but failed.

■ **Do/have a test, eg.**

- How did you **do** on your maths test?
- I'm going to **have a test** on spelling tomorrow.

■ **Sit for :** take an exam, *e.g.*

- How did you **do** on your maths test?
- I'm going to **have a test** on spelling tomorrow.

■ **Pass/fail an exam, eg.**

- Did you **pass** the exam? (Not : 'in the exam')
- No. I have **failed** my English exam.
- How did he **do** in his exams? (Do = fare)

Fare (सफल) = succeed

He **fared** well/badly in the exams.

How did you **fare** in your exams?

I passed the exams/**I did well** in the exams.

Start/Leave school (Don't say : 'the school')

Look at the examples:

- He **started** going to school at the age of four.

Leave school = stop being a student.

What would you like to do when you **leave** school?

Are you **leaving** school, John?

- **Leave the school** (विद्यालय छोड़ना)

When **'the'** is used, the meaning changes, eg :

'Leave **the** school' means, to go away from the premises.

Examples :

- The Van **leaves** the school at 2.30 in the afternoon.
- They're leaving **the** school for Delhi this evening.

Admission/admissions :

- Admission **to** this school is by examination only.
- Admissions **to** nursery clas are now closed.

Seek (to) = try to get, eg :

Q. : Which school are you **seeking** admission **to?**

Ans : I'm **seeking** admission **to** Government High School.

Apply to/for :

Q. : Which school have you **applied for** admission?

Ans : I've **applied to** a local boys' school.

Join

- He's (= he has) **joined** the Army school in Delhi.
- She is/She's thinking to **join** the modelling class.

Enroll (at/in) = enter one's name in

Enroll in (at English)

- **Say :** Do you want to **enroll** your child **in** this school?
- But you're too late to **enroll** her **at** this school.
- This school doesn't **enroll** male students.
- Could you please **enroll** her as a part-time student?

Enrollment:

- They're still waiting for **enrollment at** this school.
- School **enrollments** have crossed the limit this year.

❑❑❑

Unit-27 Talking about education (III)

(शिक्षा के बारे में बातचीत)

Describing a Child's Mental Characteristics
(बच्चे की मानसिक विशेषताओं का वर्णन करना)

Look at the examples :

- What's Malvika like? She's intelligent.
- What's Naresh like? he's a very nice boy.

Remember :

What's ..... like?

This is used to describe someone's character, ability or skill.

- **The following words can describe a child and his/her ability :**

◆ **Intelligent** (Adj.) : a child with above average mental ability is called intelligent, eg;

Intelligence (n) = The ability to learn, understand and think.

- You can measure someone's intelligence by giving him I.Q.T. eg.
- Examinations are not true measures of one's intelligence.

◆ **Brainy** (adj.) : intelligent, eg. He's brainy/she's brainy student.

◆ **Brains** (n) : intelligence, eg. She's (= she has) got more brains than physical strength.

◆ **Smart** (adj.) : clever and intelligent, eg. She's one of the smartest girls in our class.

◆ **Brilliant** (adj.) : outstanding; extremely clever or skilful at doing something, eg.

He's brilliant/he's a brilliant student/she's a brilliant dancer.

◆ **Bright** (adj.) : quick at learning; intelligent, eg. She's a bright child. Bright children should be taken care of by their parents and teachers.

◆ **Gifted** (adj.) : extremely intelligent/talented, eg. He's gifted child. Swami Viveka Nand was gifted with extraordinary powers of memory. There should be a separate school for gifted children.

◆ **Genius** (n) : a child of very high level of intelligence, eg.

She's genius (= She's a girl of very great ability)

He's a genius at mathematics/she's a genius at cards (= at playing cards).

- **Ingenious** (adj.) : very clever at making things; imaginative, cg.
  She's got an ingenious mind. Look at this toy she's (= she has) made!
- **Ingenuity** (n) : ability/cleverness at making or inventing new things, eg.
  - They were surprised at his ingenuity to work out difficult problems.
  - He'w known for his ingenuity to make and repair home appliances.
- **Creative** (adj.) : Producing new things by using one's imagination, eg.
  He's creative artist/she's creative designer.
- **Talented (adj.) :** gifted; person with a natural ability to do something well, eg.
  He's a talented physician/artist/sportsman, etc.
- **Talented** (adj.) : gifted; person with a natural ability to do somethig well, eg.
  He's a talented successian/artist/sportsman, etc.
- **Talent** (n) : A special kind of natural ability to do somethig well, eg.
  He has a talent for music/she's a girl of great talent.
- **Witty** (adj.): A clever and amusing way of saying something, eg.
  He has a witty mind.
  She's a witty girl/he's witty speaker/He passed a witty remark.

Success of a student depends on (छात्र की सफलता निर्भर करता है)

Motivation (प्रेरणा)**/aspiration** (आकांक्षा)**/initiative** (पहल)**/diligence** (परिश्रम)**/preserverance** (दृढ़ता)

- **Motivation :** something that encourages you to work harder, eg.
  - She's intelligent but lack motivation.
  - Success depends on how much motivated you are.
  - Her aim to become a doctor motivated her to work harder.
- **Aspiration :** a strong desire to do something or have something, eg.
  - Your level of aspiration will decide how far you can go ahead in life.
  - If a student has initiative, drive and energy he can achieve anything in this world.
    (Driver : a very strong desire)
- **Diligence :** hard work, eg. he has impressed his teachers with his diligence.
  - Be diligent if you want to be successful in life/he's a diligent student.

- **Perseverance :** determination to keep trying in spite of difficulties, eg.
  - Hard work and perseverance has been the chief force behind his brilliant success.
  - He showed great perseverance in getting at the top in his class.
  - Perseverance is a rare quality; It's a quality of extraordinary students.

Words used to show individual efforts and ability to get things

(व्यक्तिगत प्रयास और चीजों को पाने की क्षमता को दिखाने के लिए इस्तेमाल किये जाने वाले शब्द)

Achieve, attain, accomplish

- **Achieve :** to get or gain something by one's own efforts, eg.
  - She has/she's achieved three distinctions in her exams.
  - Getting at the top in the final exams is very hard to achieve.
- **Achievement :** Winning gold medal is a great achievement.
- **Attain :** to succeed in getting something difficult after hard efforts, eg.
  - If you want to attain your ambition, use your brain and work hard.
  - She attained great success in computer graphics by constant practice.
- **Attainment :** I consider his mastery of English language among his finest attainments.
- **Accomplish :** to finish (something) successfully; to achieve (something) :
  - Nothing can be accomplished without hard work and motivation.
  - They accomplished the task in less than half an hour.
- **Accomplishment :**
  - His getting award at the school function is no small accomplishment.
  - Her accomplishment are singing, dancing and playing the guitar.

Don't say : Good in/bad in

Say : good at / better at/genius at/clever at/poor at/ bad at, etc.

Look at the following examples :

- She's good **at** cooking but better **at** painting.
- He's good **at** physics but genius **at** maths.
- He's bad **at** writing but worse **at** spelling.
- She's poor **at** English but good **at** Hindi.
- He's very good **at** studying.

Weak at/in

- He's weak **at/in** maths.
- She's strong **at/in** languages but weak **at/in** maths.

■ The following words show mental weakness of a child

- **Stupid** : not at all sensible; lacks power of judgement, eg. Don't tourh it, you stupid!/he's stupid/she's stupid girl.
- **Dull/slow** : weak-minded; not quick at learning, eg. He's dull/slow child; her child is a bit slow in picking things up.
- **Fool** : stupid; one who behaves in a silly manner, eg. He's a fool. what fools are you talking about?
- **Silly** : stupid/brainless; behaving in a foolish or childish way, eg. – She's silly/she's a silly girl/don't do that, you silly boy!

■ Describing a child's nature (बच्चों के स्वभाव का वर्णन)

Say : What's he like? (= What kind of child is he?)
Answer : he's obedient/he's very talkative

The following words describe a child's nature :

- **Studious** = bookish/found of studying, eg. He's a studious boy.
- **Obedient** = a child who is willing to do what he is ordered to do.
- **Docile/meek/submissive :** used to describe children who are gentle and obedient.

Look at the examples :

He's very docile. (= quite and easily controlled)
She's meek and obedient child. (= very quiet and gentle)
They are very submissive when they talk to their teachers.
Note : 'submissive' children are always willing to obey.

Polite/courteous :

Polite and courteous children are well behaved, kind and respectful.

- **Confident :** a confident child can deal with a situation successfully.
- **Diffident :** a child who lacks in self-confidence. (Opp. confidant)
- **Ambitious :** an ambitious child strongly desires to be successful.
- **Aspiring :** an aspiring child wants to get something important.
- **Eager :** an eager child shows strong desire to do something.
- **Inquisitive/curious/inquiring :** These children ask too many questions. They are usually interested in too many details.
- **Quarrelsome :** a quarrelsome child is short-tempered. He often argues and picks a quarrel with somebody about something.
- **Obstinate :** a child who is difficult to deal with because he is so determined to act that no argument or persuasion can change his mind.

■ Words showng disrespect (अनादर/तिरस्कार दिखाने वाले शब्द)

- **Rude :** behaving in a manner that is not polite, eg.
  He was rather rude to me/don't be rude to your teachers/I don't like rude jokes.
- **Impertinent (ढीठ) :** rude to me/not respectful, esp. to people who are elderly.
  Such a child is too free with his tongue; shows disrespect to his teachers, eg.
  - The principal warned him for his impertinent remark/nobody likes an impertinent child.
  - He may be expelled for his impertinence. (Expelled = thrown out)
- **Insolent (बदतमीज) :** insulting; intentionally showing no respect, eg.
  - He's an insolent child/I can't tolerate his insolent behaviour.
  - He was taken to the headmaster for his insolence.
- **Impudent ;** shamelessly rude; behaves or speaks rudely or disrespectfully, eg.
  - The impudent child didn't stand when the teacher came in.
  - He has decided to punish him for his *impudence.*

■ Children causing difficulties for school authority (स्कूल प्रशासन के लिए परेशानी खड़ी करने वाले बच्चे)

- **Truant :** absentee; a student who stays away from school without permission, eg.
  - Truants often hang around (= stay out) instead of going to school.
  - She is upset because her son has been playing truant from school.
- **Bully (धमकाना) :** a boy who uses his physical power to frighten or hurt other, eg.
  - Bullies are often cowards.
  - The teacher knows well who the bullies are in the class.
  - He seems to take pleasure in bullying the younger kids.
  - be a buddy (= friend), not a bully.

❑❑❑

Unit-28 Talking about education (IV)
(शिक्षा के बारे में बातचीत)

University education (विश्वविद्यालयी शिक्षा/उच्च शिक्षा)

University : Place where students study for degrees.

Study/teach at a university

Q. : Which university do you go to (= to study)?
Ans : I'm at Delhi University (= studying at)
Q. : Which university are you at Malvika?
Ans : I am **at** Oxford.
Q. : Which university were you **at** in India, Anil?
Ans : I was at Allahabad University in the 1980.
My wife took her master's degree in 1978.

- **University/college campus** (विश्वविद्यालय/महाविद्यालय परिसर)

The land and buildings of a university or college.
Say : on/in/at university campus, eg :

- The campus **at** Allahabad University.
- Professor Gill lives **on** university campus.
- Does she live **on** campus or **in** the city?
- There's canteen **in the centre of** the campus
- The campus **at** Agra University has a big library.

- **Types of student** (छात्रों के प्रकार)

Undergraduates/Postgraduates
Undergraduates are college or university students who are studying for their **first** degree examinations. **Graduates** are students who have got their degrees. Students studying **at** colleges or universities for master's Degree of Phd. are called **Postgraduate** students.

- **Which college/university are you at?** (= as a student)

Q. : **Which** college do you go to (= attend) ?
Ans : I go to Agra College.
I'm **at** Agra College (= studying at) and my sister's **at** St John's.
I'm a law/medical/engineering student at Allahabad University.

Q. : Which university is your brother **at**?
Ans : He's **at** Shanti Niketan.
My father teaches sociology **at** a degree college in Punjab.
My mother's a lecturer **in** English **at** an intermediate college.
Q. : **Which** class are you **in** (= studying in)?
Ans : I'm in B.A. (Part-1) **at** a local college.

■ Teaching positions in a college or university
(किसी कॉलेज या विश्वविद्यालय में शिक्षण पद)

Professor (British/American English) :
'Professor' is a teacher of **the highest rank** in a department of a university.

Examples :

- He's a university professor/professor John taught us physics **at** Cambridge.
- She was a professor in physics **at** Delhi University in the 1960s.

Note : in the US 'professor' is a general term for teachers teaching at college.

- ◆ **Professorship :** the job or position of a professor in a university, eg.
He has **applied for** a professorship **in** English **at** BHU.
- ◆ **Reader :** a senior lecturer just below the position of a professor, eg.
He's a reader **in** mathematics **at** Mumbai University.
- ◆ **Readership :** the job of a reader **at** a British university or college.
- ◆ **Lecturer :** a teacher of the lowest rank in a British college/university, eg :
She was a lecturer **in** history **at** Oxford.
- ◆ **Lecturership :** the job of a lecturer (**Don't say :** Lecturership)

Look at the examples :

- He has/he's been offered a lectureship **in** physics **at** Delhi University.
- He has **applied for** lectureship **at** the University of London.

Note : in American Colleges/universities teachers are graded as assistant professor, associate professor and **professor**.
The position of a **'professor'** rank the highest.

- ◆ **Emeritus :** a retired college/university teacher.
- ◆ **Professor emeritus :** A retired professor (Honorary title)
Say : He's the professor emeritus of economics.
Mr Bose is an emeritus professor of English, etc.

Course of study (पाठ्यक्रम)

A university generally conducts courses at three levels :

Academic, Vocational and Professional

Academic courses have too much concern with theory and logic; they develop the mind rather than practical knowledge. **Vocational** courses train students for different jobs, such as secretarial work, printing, agricutlure, etc. **professional** courses include medicine, law, engineering, architecturem management, etc.

- **There are different types of courses :**

Correspondance course; Crash course; Refresher course; Sandwich course.

Correspondance/distance learning course is a course in which you get lessons through post. Crash course is a short course in which you learn only the most important things. **Refresher course** is a course that gives you knowledge about new developments in a particular subject or skill. **Sandwich course** (in Br Eng) is a course **at** a college or university in which you study and work alternately in industry or business, eg ; he's doing a four-year sandwich course in electrical engineering.

- **Qualifications** (योग्यताएँ) (often plural)

Remember : degrees awarded by a university are names of titles.

Say: Mr K. N. Seth, M.A./S. K. Pandey, M.Sc. /Ms Renu, MBA etc.

A person with a PhD degree is addressed as doctor in conversation, eg. May I speak to Dr Bose, please?

Asking about someone's qualifications

A : What are your qualifications?
B : I've got a Master's degree in journalism.
A : Do you have any qualifications in science?
B : No. I'm an arts graduate.

- **The use of a/an with a degree:**

Don't say : He's B.A/She's M.Sc, etc.

Use an indefinite article, eg. He's **a** B.A/she's **an** M.Sc.

- I'm **a** Bachelor of Arts/I'm **an** arts graduate/I'm a graduate.
- Amit's **a** postgraduate/he's (= he has) graduated from Oxford.
- She has/she's got **an** M.Sc. in Botany, etc.

Here are some more examples:

- He's a B.Tech/She's **an** M.Tech/I'm **an** MBA.

- Ravi's an LLB/She's **an** MBBS/He's **a** PhD/
- I'm **an** MS/Mr Paul is **an** FRCS, etc.

Note : The use of 'a' or 'an' before a degree (the title) depends on how it is pronounced.

Remember : a/e/f/h/i/l/m/n/o/r/s/and x begin with a vowel sound, hence take 'an', use 'a' with the rest.

■ Do/take/have/get/hold a degree

Do (= study)

Look at the examples:

- What degree did you **do** at BHU?
- I **did** B.Sc. in maths.
- What degree do you **have**? I have a degree in maths.
- Which university did you **get** it from? I got it from Cambridge.
- She holds **a** PhD in music. Where did she **take** it from?

❑❑❑

Unit-29 Choice and Preference
(पसंद और वरीयता/पसंद की वस्तु)

Making a choice (चुनाव करना)

(a) Look at the following examples :

Q. : What would you like to have? (The choice is open)

Ans : I'd like tea, please. (I'd = I would).

Remember : "What?" is used in a general sense.

"Which?" is used when there are a limited number of choices in mind.

Example: Which do you prefer- oranges or apples?

(b) Consider the following :

May I speak to Mr Banarji?

Which Banarji do you mean? We have **two** Banarjis here.

Note that 'which' is used for both persons and things, and asks for **'One'** out of a definite number, eg: Which of those men is Mr Arora?

- **Don't Say : Who is your teacher in this photograph?**

  Say : Which is your teacher in this photograph?

  Note: "Who?" is not selective, use "which" instead.

  Asking questions about something 'specific' (= particular):

  (कुछ खास चीजों के बारे में प्रश्न पूछना)

  Which road goes to the station?/Which is your favourite dish?/Which dress shall I put on?/Which is your girl friend?/Which girl is your fiancée?/Which is your favourite actress? Which hotel is the best? / Which is the way to Delhi? /Which news channels do you like most? / Which way shall we go?

  Note: a fiancee is the woman to whom a man is going to be married.

  A fiance is the man to whom a woman is engaged to be married.

  Both words are pronounced in the same way.

- **Whichever :** the one which/any one, eg.

  Take whichever you like best/whichever candidate you select, you'll have a good choice.

Which hotel would you prefer to stay in? Whichever, it doesn't matter to me.

Which day suits you? Whichever, it doesn't matter to me.

- **Asking questions (प्रश्न पूछना)**

Don't say : to which...? (Formal)

Say : Which...? (Spoken form)

Put the preposition at the end of the sentence, **eg :**

- Which school do your children go to? /Which class are you in?
- Which book are you looking for? /Which shop did you buy these shoes from?
- Which film did you go to?

- **"Which...?"**

"This' is used with a comparative/superlative degree.

Look at the examples :

- Which is the cheaper of the two hotels? /Which is the best film of this year?
- Which is farther from here- Mumbai or Calcutta? /Which is the brightest star?

- **Say : Which of?**

- Which of these two boys is more intelligent?
- Which of them is the cleverest girl?
- Which is the youngest of these boys?
- Which of you is Mr Yogi's son?

- **When...?**

This can be used to inquire about time, for example:

- When's (= when is) your birthday? Next week.
- When's your flight? Saturday evening
- When's Deepawali? Next month.

- **Which...? (More specific)**

Look at the examples:

- Which day is your birthday? 'Tuesday' (Also: What day...?)
- Which day are we celebrating the 'New year?' On Friday

Also : Which month/year...?

Expressing Preferences (वरीयता/पसंद व्यक्त करना)

Would rather (= would prefer to)

Note : 'would rather' is used to express preference, eg:

I'd (= I would) rather go (= prefer to go)

Say : How about/what about going for a swim?

Ans : I'd rather sit for a while/I'd rather take some photos.

Here are some more examples:

Come this evening.	I'd rather come tomorrow evening.
Will you have tea?	I'd rather have coffee.
Let's go swimming.	I'd rather go for a walk on the beach.
Let's sit down and gossip.	I'd rather enjoy watching TV.

Look at these examples:

Q. : **What would you rather do?** (= What would you prefer to do?')

Ans : I'd rather meet him today than wait for him till tomorrow.

Q. : How would you go to Delhi? I'd rather go by train than fly.

Ans : I'd rather not go by plain. I'd rather go by car.

Q. : Would you answer my question?

Ans : I'd rather keep quiet.

Q. : Which would you rather do (= prefer to do)?

Ans : Go to the cinema or play cricket? I'd rather play cricket.

Q. : Are you coming with us?

Ans : I'd rather not. (Spoken form)

Q. : **What would you like to be :** an engineer or a doctor?

Ans : I'd rather be a doctor than an engineer.

- **Would rather + clause**

Note : The above construction is used with two different subjects :

- The first one orders, the second follows the instructions.
- The past in the clause refers to the present or future, not the past time.

Look at the examples:

- **I'd rather** you go by plane. (=I'd prefer you to go by plane)
- I'd rather you go home. (**Don't say:** I'd rather you go home)

Note: "I'd rather you go home" is possible but very unusual.

Look at these examples :

Shall I ? (Used in offer)

- **Shall I open the window?** I'd rather you didn't if you don't mind.
- We'd rather you didn't smoke here/I'd rather you don't tell her.
- Shall I switch on TV? I'd rather you don't.
- I'd rather you come tomorrow than today.
- I'd rather you came a bit earlier.
- I'd rather your parents stay at home.

■ **Rather** = to a small extent; slightly, eg.

- The bed was **rather** uncomfortable/it's rather cold today.
- The film was **rather** boring/this book is *rather* difficult for me.
- He got **rather** suspicious and asked me to show my passport.
- She was **rather** nervous to see me in her room.

❑❑❑

Unit-30 Making comparisons

(तुलना करना)

What is Comparison? (तुलना क्या है?)

'Comparison' means how two or more things, people, ideas, etc. are similar to or different from each other. In this unit, you are going to learn how comparison is made and used in day today conversation.

The comparative:

The comparative' form of an adjective or adverb shows an increase in quality, amount or degree when compared with something else. It is usually formed by adding – **er**, for example : bigger.

More' is put before **longer** adjectives or adverbs, eg: **'More'** difficult, more interesting, more comfortable, etc. More' is occasionally used with very short adjectives.

Note : 'than' is used after comparatives.

- **As/Like:**

'As' and 'like' show similarity between people and things, situations, etc. Here are some examples:

(a) In India as in Pakistan people are very fond of spicy food.
He's (= he has) topped the university this year as his father had long ago.
She's an excellent dancer **as** her Guru used to be.

(b) The 'Shikara' looked **like** a floating house.
The twins look just **like** their mother / she looks **like** her sister.
He's very **like** his father.

- **The use of :**

As...as with adjectives/adverbs, eg :

- She's **as** intelligent as her brother/his hands were **as** cold as snow.
- Your house is **as** large **as** mine/their house **is** twice **as** large as yours.
- He practices **as** much **as** you do/he's **as** bad-tempered **as** his father.
- She's nearly **as** tall **as** her mother/your face is almost **as** round as hers.
- She works **as** hard **as** me/he looked as nervous **as** his friend.

Showing contrast

(a) Not as...as

- She's not as nice as her mother/he's **not as** kind **as** his father.
- Riding a horse is **not as** easy **as** riding a bicycle.

I don't know **as** many people **as** you /it **isn't as** hot **as** yesterday.

(b) Not so...as

Look at the examples:

- Your house is not so large as mine/your father's **not so** old as he looks.
- He's not so quick in answering as his sister/she's **not so** stupid as I thought.

Here are some more examples:

(c) Less...Than (Compare with: 'Not so...as')

- Walking is less tiring **than** running/she's **less** proud **than** her sister.
- She eats **less** food **than** her brother/this book is **less** expensive **than** yours.
- The streets were **less** crowded **than** usual/Polo is **less** popular **than** football.

(d) Much/ a little...than:

- It's **much colder** today **than** it was yesterday.
- It's **a little hotter** today **than** it was yesterday.

Comparison (formal)

Say : (a) He's **older** than **I am**.
I'm **as** strong as **he is**.

But, it is more common to say:

(b) He's **older** than **me**. (Not: I am)
I'm **as** strong as **him**. (Not: he is)

Note : if 'as' and 'than' function as prepositions, object pronouns are used. If they function as conjunctions, they are followed by a clause.

Look at these examples:

- I'm **quite tall** but you're **taller**.
- Which of you is **older**? – Me. (Not: I am)
- Which is **larger**, Delhi or Mumbai? Mumbai is **larger than** Delhi.
- How <u>old</u> is Mr Raj ?
- I don't know exactly, but he's **older than** his wife.

The same as/ different from

Look at the examples:

- Your salary is **the same as** mine/My T-shirt is **the same as** yours.
- We have **the same** brand of car, but yours is **different from** mine.
- Your son is **the same age as** me/I go to the **same** college **as** you.
- That boy's exactly **the same as** your brother.
- They look **alike** but they're quite **different from** each other.
- She's **different from** her sister/you're quite **different from** me.

More... than

Look at the examples:

- This is **more** expensive **than** that/boxing is **more** violent **than** wrestling.
- She's **more** beautiful **than** her sister/this chair is **more** comfortable **than** that.
- Going by plane is **much/a little more/a lot more** expensive **than** going by train.

Examples showing parallel increase

- **The more** you learn, **the more** modest you become.
- **The more** you earn, **the more** you spend.
- **The older** you get, **the wiser** you become.
- **The more** he drinks, **the worse** he becomes.

Examples showing gradual increase (क्रमिक वृद्धि दर्शाने वाले उदाहरण)

- The weather's getting **hotter** and **hotter** everyday.
- He's getting **more** and **more** interested in his work.
- He felt himself becoming **more** and **more** nervous.

The more... the less (examples):

- **The more** people you meet **the less** time you have for leisure.
- **The more** you work **the less** you learn.

Superlatives:

A superlative shows that a person or thing has more of a particular quality than anyone or anything else in a group. The use of 'the' is a must with superlatives.

Also: **Longer adjectives** (with two or more syllables) take **'most'** and **'least'** to form superlatives. **'Most'** means **'the largest'** number or **'the greatest'** amount of; **'least'** expresses the **'smallest'** number or amount

Look at the examples:

- Monika's the **tallest** girl. Who's the **best** student in your class?
- Our sitting room is the **most** decorated room. It's the **cleanest** room in the house.
- Amit is the **friendliest** of all my friends/I'm the second **eldest** in the family.
- Everest is the **highest** peak in the world/she's the **youngest** of them.

Here are some more examples:

Note : **'Most'** without 'the' in the following examples means 'the majority (of)'.

Tajmahal is the **most** famous building in India/**most** doctors are non-smokers.

Most people have cell-phones these days/this hotel is the **least** expensivc in Delhi/that was the **most** delicious meal I ever had/you're the **most** interesting person/travelling (in) business class on aeroplane is the **most** expensive.

I've decided to spend the **least** money on cosmetics/this room gets the **least** sunlight.

❑❑❑

Unit-31 Question Tags

(क्वेश्चन टैग)

- The knowledge and ability to use 'question tags' correctly is essential for everyone.
  the following paragraphs, tags have been discussed at length. Learn and use on extensively to make communication more effective.

  Facts about question tags:

  A question tag' is a short question attached to the end of a statement. Its purpose is to do someone whether he or she agrees with the speaker or not. 'Question tags' are commonly used in everyday speech and informal writing eg: Personal letters, novels, etc.

  In Hindi too, we have **"Hai Na?"** which is a single fixed expression and is frequently used conversation. In English, the system of tags is rather difficult and complex, but can be mastered through effort and constant practice.

- **"Isn't it?"**

  Be careful! **"Isn't it?"** cannot be the same with all forms. Also note that this question phrase' is used only when the previous statement contains the word '**is**', for example: It's very cold today, **isn't it?** (It's = it is)

- **Am I not?**

  Don't Say: Am I not?'

  Say: Aren't I?

  Note : In spoken English there is no natural short form of "Am I not?" in questions and question tags.

  Look at the examples:

Wrong	**Right**
I'm tall, am I not?	I'm tall, **aren't I**?
I'm your friend, am I not?	I'm your friend, **aren't I**?

- **Note the following:**

  A **positive** statement takes a **negative** tag; a **negative** statement takes a **positive** tag. **The auxiliaries:** am, is, are, was, and were, do, have ... etc. are repeated in the tag followed by the subject (always a pronoun)

Look at the examples:

Am/is/are:

Positive statements	**Negative statements**
I'm late today, **aren't I**?	I'm not late today, **am I**?
Monika's tall, **isn't she**?	Monika isn't tall, **is she**?
Ravi's naughty, **isn't he**?	Ravi isn't naughty, **is he**?
It's hot today, **isn't it**?	It isn't hot today, **is it**?
She's beautiful, **isn't she**?	She isn't beautiful, **is she**?
The weather's bad today, **isn't it**?	It isn't bad today, **is it**?
There's a man, **isn't there**?	There isn't a man, **is there**?
There are some trees, **aren't there**?	There aren't any trees, **are there**?
It's raining, **isn't it**?	It isn't raining, **is it**?
You're angry, **aren't you**?	You aren't angry, **are you**?
Girls are singing, **aren't they**?	Girls aren't singing, **are they**?
The weather was nice, **wasn't it**?	The weather wasn't nice, **was it**?

- **Was/were:**

Malu was at school, **wasn't she**?	Malu wasn't at school, **was she**?
The boys were hungry, **weren't they**?	The boys weren't hungry, **were they**?

- **Do/Does/Did**

You smoke cigarettes, **don't you**?	You don't smoke cigarettes, **do you**? She comes late, **doesn't she**? She doesn't come late, **does she**?
These dogs bark, **don't they**?	These dogs don't bark, **do they**?
It rained last night, **didn't it**?	It didn't rain last night, **did it**?
Amit arrived late, **didn't he**?	Amit didn't arrive late, **did he**?
You liked it, **didn't you**?	You didn't like it, **did you**?
He used to smoke, **didn't he**?	He didn't use to smoke, **did he**?

Have/Had

I've told you, **haven't I**?	I haven't told you, **have I** ?
The boys have gone, **haven't they**?	They haven't gone, **have they** ?
He has/he's arrived, **hasn't he**?	He hasn't arrived, **has he**?
Malu's got a lot of books, **hasn't she**?	She hasn't got a lot of books, **has she**?
This winter's been cold, **hasn't it**?	This winter hasn't been cold, **has it**?
He had/he'd finished the job, **hadn't he**?	He hadn't finished the job, **had he**?
He had/he'd been very ill, **hadn't he**?	He hadn't been very ill, **had he**?

■ Question tags with "have" and "do" (as full verbs)

Look at the examples:

- You have tea every morning, **don't you**? (Have= take)
- You don't have tea every morning, **do you**?

Here are some more examples :

- Amit had a blue car, **didn't he**? Amit didn't have a blue car, **did he**?
- He does cooking, **doesn't he**? He doesn't do cooking, **does he**?
- You do your duty, **don't you**? You don't do your duty, **do you**?

■ Can/Could/May/Might/Ought

I can speak English, **can't I** ?	I can't speak English, **can I**?
It could be changed, **couldn't it**?	It couldn't be changed, **could it**?
He may come, **mayn't he**?	He mayn't come, **may he**?
Malu might be at home, **mightn't she**?	Malu mightn't be at home, **might she**?
You ought to be here, **oughtn't you**?	You oughtn't to be here, **ought you**?

■ Must, Have/Has (got) to

You must go now, **mustn't you**?	You mustn't go now, **must you**?

She has to obey him, **doesn't she**? — She doesn't have to obey him, **does she**?

She's got to go, **hasn't she**? — She hasn't got to go, **has she**?

- **Will/Would/Should**

He'll come, **won't he**? — He won't come, **will he**?
Monika will go, **won't she**? — Monika won't go, **will she**?
It'll be Sunday tomorrow, **won't it**? — It won't be Sunday, tomorrow, **will it**?

You should wait, **shouldn't you**? — You shouldn't wait, **should you**?
She'd like to come, **wouldn't she**? — She wouldn't like to come, **would she**?

- **Let/Would rather**

Suggestion : Let's go for a walk, shall we?
Preference : She'd rather stay here, wouldn't she?
Note : some words as, never/seldom/rarely/scarcely are considered negative, use a positive
You never/seldom work on Sunday, **do you**?
He rarely/scarcely goes to the cinema, **does he**?

❑❑❑

Unit-32 Interrogative Sentences
(प्रश्नवाचक वाक्य)

- 'Interrogative' is the form of a sentence that asks a question. A question can be : affirmative or negative. 'Affirmative' questions can be answered in 'Yes' or 'No'.

  Forming a negative (नकारात्मक बनाना)

  In spoken English you can form a negative question by placing the contracted negative form in front of the subject, eg. Isn't he?/Aren't they?/ Can't you, etc.

- **Answers are generally short :**

  A "yes" answer shows that you agree with someone.

  "No" in the answer means you disagree with him or her. In everyday speech answer are usually short, not in full, eg :

  Do you go to school? yes, I go to school.

  No, I don't go to school.

  The above example shows an unusual way of answering a question.

  Don't say just : 'Yes' or 'No' when answering a question as it sounds rude and unfriendly, don't use the 'full form either'. An answer is full form means you want to emphasize something or express your strong feelings. The correct way is to say 'in short'.

  Look at the examples :

Questions	agreement	disagreement
Are you a student?	Yes, I am.	No, I'm not.
Are you Indian?	yes, I am.	No, I'm not.
Are you British?	Yes, I,m.	No, I'm not
Am I an actor?	Yes, you are.	No, you aren't

- **Negative questions** (नकारात्मक प्रश्न)

  Are + not + I = Aren't I? (spoken form)

  Don't say : "Am I not"

  Say : "Aren't I?"

  Remember : "Am I not?" is not the proper form of a 'negative question'.

  Consider the following

  Aren't I your friend? (**Don't say :** Am I not?)

Are't I late?/Aren't I faithful to you?

I'm your boss, aren't I?

Possible Responses : yea, you are.

Of course, you are.

No, you aren't

Note : a negative question generally expects the answer "yes".

- **Affirmative/negative questions with short answers**

Use 'contracted' form, eg.

Is + not = isn't (+ subject)

Look at the examples :

Is she a doctor? Yes, she is, No, she isn't.

Isn't she a doctor? Yes, she is. No , she isn't.

Here are some more examples :

Is it raining outside?	yes, it is.	No, it isn't
Isn't it raining outside?	Yes, it is.	No, it isn't
Is that Monika over there?	yes, it might be/yes, it could be.	

- **Are + not? = Aren't (+ subject) :**

Are they coming tommorow?	Yes, they are.	No, they aren't
Aren't they leaving tonight?	Yes, they are.	No, they aren't
Aren't the dogs barking?	Yes, they are.	No, they aren't.

- **Have + not = haven't (+ subject)**

Yet = up to now; by this/that time

Have you finished your work?	Yes I have.	No, I haven't
Haven't you finished your work yet?	Yes, I have.	No, I haven't
Have you had (= taken) your tea?	Yes I have.	No, not yet.
Haven't you had your dinner?	Yes I have.	No, I haven't
Has she got the job?	Yes, she has.	No, she hasn't.
Hasn't she got the job yet?	Yes, she has.	No, not yet.

Been to = visited, eg.

Have you ever been to Mumbai?	Oh, yes, several times/No, not really
Haven't you ever been there?	Yes, I have. No never!

- **Can/can't?**

Can you help me? Yes, I can.

Can't (+ subject)

Can't you help me? Certainly/Sorry, I can't.

- **Do + not = don't (+ subject)**

Do you like her?	Yes, I do. No, I don't
Don't you like her?	(Emphatic) of course, I do. Yes, **I do** like her Of course not
Don't you smoke?	Yeah, **I do** smoke, so what? No, I don't.
Does + not = doesn't (+ subject)	
Does he drink?	Yes, he does. No, he doesn't
doesn't he drink	(Emphatic) Yes, he **does** drink. Not at all No, he never drinks

- **Did + not = didn't (+ subject)**

Did you watch the news on TV last night	Yes, I did. No, I didn't (Emphatic) Yes, I **did** go, Oh yes, I **did** go
Didn't you go to the cinema?	No, I never go to the cinema.

- **Was + not = wasn't (+ subject)**

Was Monika absent yesterday?	Yes, she was.	No, she wasn't
Wasn't she absent yesterday?	Yes, she was.	No, she wasn't

- **Were + not = weren't (+ subject)**

Were the dog hungry?	Yes, they were.	No they weren't
Weren't the dogs hungry?	Yes, they were. I think so.	No they weren't I don't think so.

- **Question with 'will' and 'would'**

Look at the examples :

Will + not = won't (+ subject)

Will he come tomorrow?	Yes. He will/No, he won't
Will there be a flower show this evening	May be, I don't know.
Won't he come tomorrow?	Yes, he will/No, he won't

Would + not = wouldn't (+ subject)

Look at the examples :

Would you have (= take) some tea	Thank you. (= Yes, I want) No, thanks (= No, I don't want)
Wouldn't you have some tea?	Thank you/No, thanks

Unit-33 Your food (I)
(आपका भोजन/खाना)

- **The three meals :**

People normally eat three times a day : in the morning, at midday and in the evening. The morning meal is **breakfast;** the meal you eat in the middle of the day is called **lunch** and the meal taken in the evening is dinner.

- **Dinner** (रात का खाना)

'Dinner' is the **main meal** (= heavy food) of the day. It also means a **formal meal** given on a **special occasion** in **the evening,** eg : A dinner party. If **dinner** (heavy food) is eaten **at midday,** the **food** in **the evening** is called **supper;** the **midday meal** is called **lunch** if you take **dinner** in **the evening**.

- **Meal time**

Look at the examples :

- Busy people never forget to meet **at** meals.
- Regular mealtime keeps you fit.

A meal can be :

Simple; square; light; heavy; hot or cold

Old people prefer **simple** and **light** meal; a **heavy** meal is difficult to digest. people don't like **cold** meal; they like **hot** meal because it is **tasty and** appetizing. A **square** meal is **decent** and a **healthy** meal.

- **Look at these words : Cook/prepare/make**

You **make** a drink/tea/ coffee, etc. You **make** a meal : breakfast/lunch/dinner. make means, **'prepare'**, eg :
You make (= cook) a meal by **heating** (baking/frying/boiling).

- **Breakfast can be : large/small/good**

Remember : 'breakfast' is the **first** meal of the day.
It can be **large** or **small**.
Example : He has (= eats) a **large/big** breakfast.
Large = more than the average amount

Look at the examples :

- Does he have **a good** breakfast (= a good amount of ....)?
- A farmer doesn't have **a small** breakfast. He has **a big** breakfast this morning.

  I've **had** (= eaten) my breakfast.

  He'd **had** (= eaten) **a good** breakfast before you arrived.

Note : 'Have' can mean eat/drink/take and can be used in all tenses.

■ **Breakfast can be :** heavy or light

Say : I ate a heavy breakfast this morning. (Heavy = large)

She eats **a light** breakfast. She's slimming.

■ Cook/make a breakfast

Examples :

- She cooks a light breakfast for her kids.
- After washing she **made** us a hot breakfast.

■ At breakfast :

- Don't disturb me when I'm **at breakfast** (= eating breakfast)
- Mr and Mrs Yogi were **at** breakfast when we arrived.

Could I speak to Amit, please? Sorry, he's **at** breakfast.

Say : for breakfast

Take tea/coffee/biscuit, etc. **for** breakfast. **(don't say :** in breakfast)

Look at the examples :

What's (= what is) **for** breakfast?/Can't I have some coffee **for** breakfast.

She usually has (= takes) a cup of tea and toast **for** breakfast.

Ask someone :

What would you like **for** breakfast? (= What do you want for ....?)

Response : I'd like some tea and cake, please. (I'd = I would)

Likewise : **for** lunch, **for** dinner .... etc. **(don't say :** in lunch/dinner...)

Look at the examples :

I'd like some coffee and fried potatoes **for** lunch. (I'd like = I want)

What would you **like** to have **for** dinner/supper?

■ Here are some words and phrases

(a) Go to/go out to/go for/ take to

Examples :

- He's (= he has) gone **to** lunch/he's gone out **to** lunch.
- He's gone **for** lunch/I took him out **to** lunch.

Note : 'to' refers to the place (outside); 'for' suggests the 'purpose'.

(b) Invite to/for

- He invited his boss **to** lunch/he's gone out **to** lunch.
- I invited her **to** tea/he sent out invitation **to** a dinner party.
- We have invited them **for** dinner **at** eight this evening.
- Also : They're coming **for** dinner **at** eight this evening.
- **Invite to :** request someone to a meal (at your place)
- **Invite for :** request for a meal.

(c) Give/hold/have

- The president's **giving** dinner **to** the visiting prime minister.
- He **gave** a cocktail party **on** the opening ceremony of this shop.
- He's **giving** dinner **on** his fiftieth wedding anniversary.
- Mr and Mrs Verma are **holding** a lunch party next week.
- We're **having** a dinner **at** a posh hotel.

(a) At/ in/ over/ for

Look at the examples :

- I saw him **at** the restaurant/he waited **for** me **at** the cafe.
- She danced **at** the party/the president gave a speech **at** the dinner.
- He **took** lunch in the hotel they were **dining in** the restaurant.
- We met **over** dinner/spent an hour **over** dinner. (over = during)
- They sorted out their differences over dinner.
- Shall we meet over lunch?

Note : use **'at'** if you are using the name of a building.

'At' is used for group activities, eg. **At** a party/concert, etc.

'In' means **'inside'**.

(b) At tea/lunch/dinner :

- **Could** I speak to your father? Sorry, he's **at tea** (= drinking tea)
- They were **at lunch** when I arrived. (= Eating lunch)
- I was **at dinner** when the phone rang. (= Eating dinner)

■ Learn the following words

◆ **Buffet :** food or drink are eaten **at** a party.

- In a buffet system guests he or she themselves and standing up.

  Example : I met him after years **at** a buffet lunch.

  Note : "T" is not pronounced in 'buffet'.

Look at the examples :

- The committee **gave** a buffet lunch after the speech.
- We're going to **have** a buffet lunch after the speech.

◆ **Luncheon :** a formal lunch usually **given** in honour of a high official, e.g. –
The Mayour was present **at** a private luncheon.

◆ **Business lunch :** mid-day meal **at** which business is discussed, eg. He arranges business lunches at expensive hotels.

▪ Look at these words :

◆ **Brunch**
A late morning meal (= a combination of breakfast and lunch)

- On Sunday we got up late and ate hot brunch instead of breakfast.
- Brunches were served to the guests **on the train** (= in the train)

Dessert :
Course of fruit, ice cream, etc, served **at the end of** a meal, eg.

- There's ice cream **for** dessert/**Could** I see the dessert menu please?
- Menu = a list of dishes (all the food)

◆ **Refreshment** (अल्प आहार/जलपान)
This refers to **a small amount of** food and drink taken **at** different intervals, e.g. –

- After the parade the cadets were **provided with** some light refreshments.

◆ **Treat :**

- You entertain someone **with** food or drink, eg. I gave him a treat.
- He took his friend out **for** dinner as **a birthday treat**.
- "Keep your money away; it's my turn **to treat** you today. "
(Keep your money away = don't pay this time)

◆ **Snack(s) :**
Snacks are small, light things eaten between main meals.
Sandwiches, omelettes, **cakes,** biscuits, samosas, etc. are snacks.

Look at these examples :

- Parents should discourage children to eat surgary snacks.
- Would you like some snacks?/Is there a snack bar near here?

◆ **Snack bar :** a place when snacks can be eaten or bought to take away.

❑❑❑

Unit-34

Your food (II)

(आपका भोजन/खाना)

Types of food (भोजन के प्रकार)

Food can be rich or poor. **Rich** food is fatty.

- **Fatty** food contains a lot of **fat** in it. **Poor** food is **low** in quality.
- **Greasy food :** This type of food is covered with greasy : a thick **oily** substance.
- **Saturated food :** This kind of food makes your stomach uncomfortably **full**.
- **Junk food : chemically** treated **unhealthy** food; it contains a lot of fat, sugar, etc:
  Some people are habitual of eating a lot of **junk** food only to get ill.
- **Moreish food :** very **tasty food** they you want to eat a lot.
- **Savoury food :** refers to food with a **salty taste.**

■ **The food you eat can be** (आप जो खाना खाते हैं वह हो सकता है) : **Delicious, spicy, hot in taste, pungent, bitter.**

- **Delicious :** food that is delicous is very **pleasant** to **taste** and **smell**.
- **Opposite :** coarse food (ordinary food).
- **Spicy :** food that gives you a **pleasantly** strong **burning** feeling.
- **Opposite :** Plain (non-flavoured).
- **Hot in taste :** something like chilli, cayenne, mustard, pepper, etc. This kind of food has a **strong burning** taste because of **spices**.
- **'Hot'** means : causing **burning sensation** on the tongue.
- **Pungent :** something strong, **sharp** smelling and **unplesant** in **taste**. Cloves and garlic fall into this category.
- **Bitter :** something that is **sharp** and **unplesant** in **taste,** eg :
- **A bitter** pill; a **bitter** medicine; a **bitter** tasting liquid, etc.

The food you eat can be : Over-cooked/under-cooked/salty or saltless.

■ **Preserved/frozen/tinned food** (संरक्षित/जमा हुआ/डिब्बा बंद)
Food of this kind is kept safe for future use.

- **Preserved food :** this type of food is preserved by way of freezing drying and pickling.
- **Jams, chutneys,** etc. are examples of this type.

- **Frozen food :** this kind of food is preserved at a very low temperature.
- **Tinned food :** a kind of food that is preserved in a tin by sealing it.
- **Also :** 'fast food' meaning : already prepared hot food that can be served quickly if ordered.

■ **Diet (आहार) :** a special kind of food.

Your diet should be : balanced/healthy/diet.

Types of diet : (आहार के प्रकार)

1. Vegetarian diet, non-vegetarian diet, liquid diet, high-fibre diet, nutritious diet.
2. Low-fat diet, salt-free diet, low-salt diet, high protein diet, crash diet.
3. High calorie diet, low calorie diet, calorie-controlled diet.

Look at the examples :

- Are you **on** a diet? / Has yor doctor **put** you **on** a diet?
- If you are **dieting** what sort of **diet** are you taking?

■ **Food that has gone 'bad' (खाना जो खराब हो गया हो)** (= spoiled)

The following words can be used to describe 'spoiled food' (= unfit to eat)

Stale, sour, rancid, mouldy, rotten

- **Stale (बासी) :** this kind of food is not fresh; it is tasteless, unplesant in smell and dry.
- **Sour (खट्टा) :** something that tastes like a **lemon** or an **unripe** sour apple.
- **Rancid (बासी/विकृत गंध) :** this word is used for **fatty foods** like ghee, butter, etc. that have gone bad.
  Such food is **ill** smelling and **unpleasant** in taste.
- **Rotten (सड़ा हुआ) :** fruit, vegetables, eggs, etc. that have **gone bad** (= decayed)

■ **How to use the following words :**

Feel/taste/go/become/turn

Examples :

- This bread **feels/tastes** stale. It is **getting/becoming** stale.
- It has/it's **gone** stale. The milk has **turned/become** sour.
- Coffee **goes** stale withing a couple of weeks. How does it feel, fresh or stale?
- Intense heat has turned this milk sour/this ghee has **gone** bad.

Sour/mouldy/rancid :

- These grapes have become **sour**/this food has become partly **mouldy**.
- Don't eat this **rancid** butter; it smells/tastes **unplesant**.
- **Oily/fatty** food that has become **rancid** smell unpleasant.

Look at these examples :

- **Have/take** a smell of this bread and tell me whether it's stale.
- Don't eat this **mouldy** bread/this ghee has **become** mouldy.
- These eggs have **gone** rotten/this milk has **gone** sour.
- It's **mouldy**. I don't like its **nasty** smell. (= horrible smell)
- Several people fell ill after eating **rancid** food.

■ Tastes and flavours (स्वाद और सुगंध)

Consider the uses of the following words and expressions :

(a) Taste : Please **taste** this chocolate.
How does it **taste**?
It is/it's **sweet**. it has a sweet taste. It *tastes* sweet.

(b) Taste of : (Used to suggest a particular flavour)
Examples : This soup **tastes of** garlic.
This chutney **tastes of** ginger.

(c) Taste like : (Used to inquire about taste of something)
Say : What does sugar **taste like**?
It **tastes** sweet. (= it's sweet)

(d) To the taste : **Say :** Honey is **sweet** (to the taste)
Lemon is sour **to the taste**.
This pill is bitter **to the taste**.

(e) To taste : to try a bit of (something)
He offered him the wine **to taste**.

(f) To taste : (as much as is needed)
After cooking, add salt **to taste**.

(g) Have a taste of : (a request to taste)
Will you **have a taste of** this pudding?
Won't you **have a taste of** this pudding?

Asking and answering questions

- **Look at this putter :**

  Q. : What does it **look like?**

  Ans : It **looks** stale. It **looks like** stale butter.

- **Feel this bread**

  Q. What does it **feel like?**

  Ans : It **feels** stale. it **feels like** stale bread.

- **Smell this ghee**

  Q. What does it **taste like?**

  Ans : It **smells** rancid. It **smells like** rancid ghee.

- **Taste this milk**

  Q. What does it **taste like?**

  Ans : It **tastes** sour. It **tastes like** sour milk.

- **Look like**

  Q. What does it **look like?**

  Ans : It **looks** like lemon. Perhaps, it's lemon.

  But it doesn't **taste like** lemon. Lemon **tastes** sour doesn't it?

  Yes, it does.

- **Taste like**

  Q. : What does honey **taste like?**

  Ans : It **tastes** sweet.

  Lemon doesn't **taste** sweet. Honey doesn't **taste** sour.

  Lemon <u>neither</u> **tastes** sweet <u>nor</u> honey **sour**.

  They <u>both</u> taste **sour** and **sweet**.

❑❑❑

Unit-35

Going for Shopping
(खरीदारी के लिए जाना)

Let's talk about shop, store and supermarket where goods are kept and sold. People frequently visit these places to buy things of their daily **need.** The present unit deals with shopping, shoppers and the connected words and expression.

- **Shop/Store/Supermarket** (दुकान/गोदाम/सुपर मार्केट)

I'm going to **the shops**. (Br English)
I'm going to **the store**. (Am English)
Don't say 'the stores'

Look at the following examples :

- You go to **the shoe shop** to buy shoes/**the bookshop** to buy books, etc.
- Mother goes to the store **at/on** the weekend to buy **groceries.**

Note : **'at** the week end' (Br English)/ **'On** the weekend' (Am English)
Groceries = food and small items for the house.
They are sitting **in the shop/**there's a **repairing shop** next to the post office.
I bought it from **the clothing shop**/fresh onions **are** available **in the store now**.

Department store (not departmental) (डिपार्टमेंट स्टोर/विक्रय भंडार)

She works in a department store in London.
Note : **'Store'** in American English, and **'Shop'** in British English are the usual words for the place that sells different kinds of things. In British English a very **large shop** is called a **department store.** It is divided into different departments that sell many different things. A **supermarket** is a **large shop** where all kinds of food, drinks and other things are sold.

Remember : in spoken English people don't normally say :

- I'm going to the grocer's shop.
- She went to **the hairdresser's. (Don't say :** hairdresser's shop)
- He's gone to **the chemist's**/I bought these shoes **at the Bata's**.
- I've got an appointment **at the doctor's** at 6.30.
- She went to **the doctor's** yesterday.

- **Shopping mall/Plaza :**

These are places where people go to buy things.

- **'Shopping mall'** is a large enclosed shopping centre, eg.
  There are about fifty shops in the 'New Mall' near Gandhi Park.
- **'Plaza'** is an open place in a city.
  It also refers to a group of buildings including shops.

Shopping street/shopping corner

Area in a city where a lot of shops have been built close together.

- **Shopper** (n) : a person who is shopping, eg.
  - Shops are packed with shoppers on Christmas Eve.
  - There were large crowds of shoppers in the streets.

Note : 'eve' is the 'day' before an important occasion.

- **Shopping bag/shopping cart**

Shopping bag : a bag to carry shopping (things)

A 'Shopping cart' (to carry groceries)

Groceries : things to be sold by a grocer.

Shopping (n) = purchases (the items/things bought in shops), eg.

Shopping is carried on trolleys in large stores.

Are you tried? Let me carry your shopping.

Put the shopping in this bag, please.

- **Learn the following words and expressions :**

Shop/shopping/do the shopping/go shopping/shop around

Look at the examples :

(a) Shop (v) : to buy things, eg.

She went to market **to shop** but didn't buy anything.

I was **shopping** for a new gown at Palika Bazaar.

People usually **shop** on Sunday, but I don't.

They prefer **to shop** at the footpath stalls.

She's (= she has) **shopped** at the locak market for years.

(b) Shopping (n) : the activity of visiting shops, eg.

In London some markets are open for late night **shopping**.

I don't like **shopping** at supermarkets. They're much crowded.

You need a lot of money for **shopping** in Delhi.

(c) Do the shopping : Visiting the shops to buy things, eg.

- We haven't **done** Deepawali/Christmas **shopping** yet.
- My mother **does the shopping** thrice a week.
- Does your cook **do the shopping** everyday?
- I'll **do the shopping** tomorrow.

(d) Go shopping :

The most commonly used phrase in spoken English.

It means : **'Go to shops'** to buy things you need regularly.

Don't say : I went for shopping yesterday.

Say : I went shopping yesterday.

Note : 'go shopping' is used without 'for'.

Here are some examples :

- I'm **going shopping** because I want to buy some presents.
- She's **gone shopping.** (= She has gone out to the shops)
- When does she **go shopping**? She **goes shopping** after lunch.
- How often do you **go shopping? I go shopping** twice a week.
- Let's **go shopping** together. I want to buy some clothes.
- We're **going shopping** in London this evening.
- I've got to **go shopping** after breakfast this morning.
- We and The Guptas **went shopping** at Kingston yesterday.

(e) Shop around : compare prices by visiting different shops, eg.

- Shop around before you decide which suit fits you perfectly.
- Shop around for the best deal when you're buying jewellery.

■ Learn the following words :

◆ **Shoplifting** (n) : the crime of stealing from a shop, eg :
The woman with blue eyes was charged with shoplifting.

◆ **Shoplift** (v) : to take something from a shop without paying for it, eg.
They caught him shoplifting. Later he was handed over to the police.

◆ **Shoplifter** (n) : A person who steals things from a shop, eg.
Shoplifters are under video **surveillance** in this store. (Observation)
Shoplifters will be prosecuted if caught shoplifting.

❑❑❑

Unit-36 Asking How Much Thing Cost
(वस्तुओं की कीमत पूछना)

This unit deals with the language used in shopping situations – going to shops to buy things, making and answering queries, bargaining, etc. Connected words and expressions have been used in detail to make the learner's communication more effective. Besides, dialogues exchanged between people in situation like paying bills, rents, fares, etc. make this until all the more useful to the learner.

- **Price/cost/charge/rent/fare**

Price : the amount of money that you pay for buying something, **eg.**

- Food **prices** are **rising** steadily (= regularly)
- Don't **sell** your bike **so cheap.** Wait fot the **right** price.
- He **sold** his house at **a good price/**computer **price** have been **falling**.
- Fuel **Prices** are not **stable** in this country. Overall the **trend** is upward.
- Some companies are going to offer big **price cuts** at Deepawali.
- Don't buy from these shops. Their **prices** are **too high**.
- You can get (= buy) air conditioners at **low price** these days.

- **Different ways of asking and saying how much things cost**

(चीजों की कीमत कितनी है यह पूछने और कहने के विभिन्न तरीके)

Cost : the amount of money needed for buying, doing or producing something.

Look at thse examples :

(a) The commonest way of asking about price is to say :

How much is this? (= How much does this cost)

How much is that? (= How much does that cost)

Response : It is/it's fifty rupees/that's thirty rupees a kilo, etc.

Look at these examples :

Q. : **How much is this blue shirt?**

Ans : **It is/it's** 390 rupees. (= **It costs** 390 rupees)

Q. : **How much** is the sugar? (= **What price** is a kilo of sugar?)

Ans : **It is/It's** 50 rupees a kilo/**It's** 50 rupees per kilo. (Per = for each ...)

Q. : **How much** is that coat with the white collar?

Ans : **It is/It's** 175 rupees.

Q. : **How much** are the bed sheets?
Ans : They're 75 rupees each.
Q. : **How much** are these socks?
Ans : They 're 75 rupees a pair.
Q. : **How much** are the shoes?
Ans : They're 490 rupees.

▪ At the Greengrocer's

Don't say : At the Green grocer's <u>shop</u>

Note : A greengrocer is a person who **sells** fruit and vegetables.

Conversation :

Customer : I'd like half kilo of apples, please.
How much is it?
Greengrocer : That's 17 rupees.
Customer : Here you are. (= Here is the money)
How much is 2.5 kilos of peas?
Greengrocer : Thirty five rupees (= it is/It's 35 rupees)
Customer : Here's the money.
Greengrocer : Thanks.
Customer : How much are the bananas?
Greengrocer : That's 24 rupees a dozen.
Customer : How much are lemons and oranges?
Greengrocer : The lemons are 50 paise each; oranges are 20 rupees a kilo.
How much do you want?
Customer : Give me six oranges and three lemons, plesae.

▪ Buy (for) :

I bought half kilo of butter <u>for</u> Rs. 65/sugar 1 kg <u>for</u> 20 rupees/peas 2 kg <u>for</u>16 rupees/green onion <u>for</u> 19 rupees/a pair of socks <u>for</u> ten rupees.

Say : How much money did I pay <u>to</u> the shopkeeper?

▪ Learn these words : reduction, discount

Look at the examples :

There's a slight reduction <u>in</u> the price of food grains.

- **Reduction** <u>in</u> the price is possible if you buy <u>in</u> bulk.
  I got this mobile set <u>at</u> the **reduced** price.
- **Discounts** <u>on</u> the food items are not given <u>at</u> this shop.
  I bought this suit <u>at</u> a 10% **discount** (= he discounted 10%)

You can buy things here <u>at</u> **discount** rates.

I'm a senior citizen. Will you **give** me a **discount?**

We give five percent discount <u>for</u> cash payment.

- **Here are some more words and expressions :**

(a) Bargain : You **bargain** (= discuss) <u>with</u> a person <u>for</u> something, **eg.**

- They **bargained** <u>with</u> the farmers <u>for</u> a supply of fresh vegetables.
- You **bargain** <u>with</u> a shopkeeper <u>over</u> price of something.
- You buy something <u>at</u> **bargain** price (= at a lower price)
  After a successful business deal (= agreement)
  You say : "In many ways it was **a good bargain.**"

(b) Haggle (मोलभाव करना) : You agrue with someone <u>about/over</u> price of something.

Note : 'haggle' is almost the same as bargain, eg.

- Women are terrific buyers. They don't buy anything without **haggling**.
- He was **haggling** <u>with</u> the rickshaw puller <u>over</u> the fare.
- The old lady bought a Chinese umbrella after a lot of **haggling**.
- It's traditional to haggle <u>over</u>/<u>about</u> the price of things in India.

Learn these words :

Cash down (= paying at once); **Dear** (= expensive)

Conversation : (Buying the house)

Client : How much is this house, Mr Tom?

Mr. Sen : It/it's <u>over</u> 16 lakh, 15 lakh if you pay cash down. That's a reasonable price for this lovely house.

Client : That's true, but the price is too **dear** for me.

Mr. Sen : That's a special price for you. You can **move into** the house next week if you want to.

Client : But, It's too much; I can't buy it <u>at</u> this price.

Mr. Sen : Well, here's my last offer; 14 lakh.

Client : I can't manage more than 13 lakh.

Mr. Sen : OK, see you tomorrow, good bye!

- **At the hotel**

Charge : money asked for goods/services, eg :

How much do you **charge** <u>**for**</u> a single room?

(Or) **How much** is a single room?

Conversation

Mr. Tom : How much are the rooms, please?
Receptionist : A single room's 125 rupees.
Mr. Tom : How much is a double room?
Receptionist : It's hundred and fifty rupees.
Mr. Tom : How much do you **charge** for a night?
Receptionist : three hundred rupees a night.

Note : a double room is a bedroom for two people.

Learn these words :

Bill, rent (out), hire (out), hire purchase,
Charter, fare, fee/fees

Note : 'bill' is a list showing how much you have to pay for something.

Below are some questions and answers :

Q. : How much was the **bill** for dinner?
Ans : It was over 350 rupees.
The **bill** for dinner **came to** over three hundred and fifty rupees.
Q. : Have you paid the **bill?**
Ans : Not yet. Could I have the **bill,** please?
Q. : How much did the **bill come to?** (= amount to/reach)
It **came to** Rs. 1500/- I didn't expect the **bill to come to** so much.
He **got** his damaged car **repaired** yesterday. How much did he pay for it?

Rent (किराया) (v) :

You pay/receive money for the use of a room/house, eg.
He rented a room/house/car, etc.

Look at these examples :

- I've rented this house from Mr. Kapoor/these rooms rent at Rs. 2500 a month.
- She's (= she has) **rented** this room to us/we live in a **rented** flat.

Rent (to/out) :

To let someone live in a house for money, eg. (Let = to allow)

- She wants to **rent out** her flat.
- He **rents out** the rooms to students.

Rent (n) :

- Payment of money for using land/building/machinery, etc. eg :
- This is a **rent free** house/this house is for **rent**/how much is its **rent**?

- Office **rents** are extremely **high** in some parts of Delhi.
- **You pay :** a high/heavy/low rent.

■ **Hire** (out) : you hire something for just a short period.

Examples :

- How much will I have to pay if I **hire** a car for a fortnight?
- Taxis are **hired out** to foreign tourist by travel agencies.
- Some dealers indulge in **hiring out** blue films.
- We're **hiring** catering at the weeing reception.
- How much would you have to pay for it?

Hire purchase : (Installment plan), eg.

- It's more expensive to get domestic items on **hire purchase**.
- He's bought the latest model of a diesel-powered car on **hire purchase**.

■ **Charter :** to hire (= rent) buses, ships or planes for use, *e.g.* –

- The US Red Cross has **chartered** a plane to carry supplies to boarder areas.
- The **chartered** plane crashed/she was travelling on a **chartered** plane.
- How much did you pay for the **chartered** flight?

■ **How much is the fare?** (किराया कितना है?)

Fare : the price/cost you pay to travel by bus, train, plane, *e.g.* –

- How much is the bus **fare** from Agra to Delhi? Train **fares** are going up again.
- Bus **fares** have **risen** by 15% this year. He spends Rs. 300/- a month on fares.
- In Delhi buses are very cheap. **Fares** are from 5 to 7 rupees for any distance.
- Trains to Delhi run from 6 am and the first class **fare** is 350 rupees.

■ **Fee/fees** (शुल्क) **: (usually 'fees')**

'Fee' is money paid for professional advice or services, eg.

A lawyer or doctor **charges** fee for their professional services.

Say : School fees/entrance fees/consultancy fees/registration fees/licence fees.

Note : License fees (Am Eng)

❑❑❑

Unit-37 Talking About Clothes (1)

(कपड़े के बारे में बातचीत)

Clothes : Things that you wear

Men in our country wear light clothes, such as : dhoti, kurta, pajamas, shirts, etc. Women usually wear 'Sari' – a long piece of clothing, blouse, petticoat, etc. The word **'clothes'** has **singular**, it is used only in the **plural** form followed by a **plural** verb. Your shirt is not a **'clothe'** but an article of **'clothes'**. What you are wearing at the moment are all **articles** of clothes. Words such as : **article/item/thing** can be used with **clothes** or **clothing**.

- **Clothes/Clothing** (कपड़े/वस्त्र)

  There is a difference between 'clothes' and 'clothing'
  Clothing (collective) is a **formal** word for **'clothes'**. it refers to **all** the **clothes** a person has or wearing. **'Clothing'** also refers to a **particular** type of clothes, eg : **protective** clothing, **waterproof** clothing, **synthetic** clothing, etc.

  Consider the following examples :

  - They urgently need several **warm** article of **clothing**.
  - Prices of **clothing** fell articles of **clothing**.
  - prices of **clothing** fell by five percent last month.
  - Food, **clothing** and shelter are our priority.
  - **Deep** sea drivers need **protective** clothing.

- **(a) Cloth :**

  Don't confuse the two words : **'cloth'** and **'clothes'** as they are not the same.
  'Clothes' are tailor-made; where as **'cloth'** is the **woven** material of which **"clothes"** are made.

  Look at the examples :

  - How much **'cloth'** do you need to make **a pair of** trousers?
  - The **cloth** you've bought is **a little short for your coat.**
  - I need 2.5 meters of **cloth** to meke your **pants** (plural).

  (b) Cloth (n) : piece of cloth for a particular purpose
  Cloths (plural) : separate **clothes** are used for clearing household things.

Look at the examples :

- You mop up (= wipe) sauce that's been spilt with **a bit of** old **cloth**.
- I use **a damp cloth** for rubbing stains/**floor cloth** is used for clearing.
- You **wipe** the surface with **a dry cloth/a tablecloth** is used for covering.
- Can I use this **dishcloth** to wipe the dishes?

■ **Clothe (v)** (कपड़े पहनना/पहनाना) : **= to provide with clothes; dress, e.g.**

- You need a lot of money **to feed** and **clothe** your family these days.
- A partially **clothed** dead body was found lying in a pool of blood.
- The Neta **clothed** in the white dhoti and kurta came on the stage.
- He was **clothed** in a blue suit/she followed him **clothed** in a sari.

■ **Learn the following words :**

Clotheir (बुनकर, जुलाहा) **:** dealer in cloth/clothes.

Manufacturer : a company or industry that design and manufacture clothes or material for clothes.

Cloth-merchant : (a) a wholesale dealer/suplier.
(b) Person trading in clothes.

Clothing industry : industry manufacturing cloth or clothes.

Clothes shop : a shop where clothes are sold, e.g.
There are a number of clothes shops at Chandni Chowk in Delhi.

■ **Dress materials** (पोशाक सामग्री) **:** Cloth/fabrics such as : cotton, wool
There are used to make dresses/clothes, curtains, etc.

Look at the examples :

- One and a half metres of **material** is enough for the trousers.
- What kind of **material** shall we buy for the curtains?
- How much of **material** is needed for a woolen suit?
- What **material** is your jacket made of?

■ **Learn the following words and phrases :**

- **Roll of cloth :** It means a piece of cloth/material which has been rolled into a tube.
- **Roll up :** If the shopkeeper rolls up a piece of cloth, he folds it several times.
- **Roll out :** He rolled (= spread out) a piece of cloth for the customer to look at.

- **Unroll** : To open from a rolled position
  e.g. : He unrolled the cloth for us to have/take a close look at it.
- **Wrap** : fold/roll up,
  e.g. : He wrapped up all the saris before closing the shop.

■ Garment (परिधान/पोशाक)

A formal word use for a piece of clothing : shirt, coat, frock, etc.

- **Ready-made garments:** Clothes made in standard sizes to be sold at clothes shop.
- **Winter garments** : Clothes that you wear in winter.
- **Summer garments** : Worn in summer.

■ Fancy : expensive/fashionable (फैंसी : महंगा/फैशनेबल)

Fancy items : very expensive saris/shawls/dresses/buttons, *e.g.* Fancy items with fancy work are sold at fancy shop.

Fancy work : embroidery; ornamental sewing, etc.

■ Colourful : having bright colour or different colours, *e.g.*

The children in colourful dresses present at the function.

■ Here are some more words to learn :

Colourfast; coloured; washable

- **Colourfast :** clothes that don't lose colour when washed, *e.g.* Is this sari colourfast?/this **suiting** is colourfast.
  Note : 'suiting' is fabric/material (= cloth) used for making men's suits.
- **Coloured :** having a colour, eg. She wore a **multi-coloured** dress. He was looking very smart in his **cream-coloured** suit.
- **Washable :** a peace of cloth/clothes that can be washed in water, *e.g.*
  - Kashmiri shawls and blankets are warm and washable.
  - Are these silken sheets and covers washable?

■ Look at these words :

School wear/sportswear/swimwear/men's wear/women's wear/children's wear.

Note : 'wear' at the end refers to a piece of clothing.

Here are some more words :

- **Underwear :** underclothing (worn under a suit, dress, etc.)
  Bra/panties/tight fitting shirts : these are women's underclothing.
- **Lingerie :** refers to underclothing/nightdresses worn by women in bed.

- **Maternity wear :** clothes for women who are going to have a baby.
- **Hosiery :** socks, underwear and tights (clothes that are tight fit)
- **Knitwear :** knitted garments (scarf, jumper, knitted shawls), etc.
- **Summer wear :** suitable to wear in the summer.
- **Evening wear :** suitable to wear in the evening.

■ **Some clothes are made of two parts of the same size and shape, eg.**

Trousers, pants, knickers, panties, jeans, pajamas, shorts, etc.

Clothes of this type are **plural** in number hence; take a 'plural' verb, eg.

My trousers **are** too long/where **are** my jeans?/your panties **are** too tight.

Note : 'trousers' in Br English is the same as 'pants' in Am English.

■ **Pair (जोड़ा) (of)**

Say : a pair of jeans; two pairs of trousers, etc.

Look at the examples :

- There are **three** pairs of pajamas in my wardrobe/I want **a** new pair of trousers.
- He bought **two** pairs of pants at a clearance sale.
- She has at least **five** pairs of jeans.
- A **smartly** dressed man came to see you when you were not here.
- The Pandal was full of **well-dressed** ladies/the waiters were **neatly** dressed.
- **Get dressed;** we're late for the party.
- The boy **dressed in** blue suit is my friend. (Dressed in = wearing)

■ **Dress up (अच्छे कपड़े पहनना) :** put on clothes (for a formal occasion), *e.g.*

- He **dressed up** for the wedding/the children **dressed up** as soldier.
- We all **dressed up** for the birthday party.

■ **Get dressed (कपड़े पहनना, तैयार होना) :** put on clothes, *e.g.*

- He **had** a bath, **got dressed** and rushed out.
- **Get dressed**; they're just arriving.

■ **Undress (वस्त्रहीन) :** if you undress, you "take off" your clothes, *e.g.*

- He **undressed**/got **undressed** (= threw all his clothes down)
- She **undressed** the doll and **put** a new dress **on** her.

■ **Have on :** (be) wearing something, *e.g.*

- He **had on** the old suit/the kurta he **had on** was too big.

- She **had** nothing **on** except a torn sari. (Had on = wore)
- Have a shawl **on** or you'll **get/catch** a cold.

■ **'Costume' means : (पोशाक/परिधान)**

Woman's suit :

(a) Short coat and skirt (of the same material)

(b) Clothes related to a particular country/period of history, *e.g.* All the dancers at the procession were in Rajasthani costumes.

(c) Clothes worn by peopoe of a particular place, *e.g.* They were present at the stadium in their national costumes.

■ **There is a difference between 'put on' and 'wear'**

'Put on' refers to the act.

'wearing' shows what you are having on (now)

Look at the examples :

- He's **putting** a piece of clothing **on** (a part of his body) **Wearing** (= is having on) something, *e.g.*
- He's **wearing** a dhoti and kurta (now)
- He **wore** a suit (= had a suit on) when he came to see me.
- People **wear** (= have on) cotton clothes in the summer.

■ **Putting on/taking off clothes (कपड़े पहनना/उतारना)**

◆ **Put on :** put a piece of clothing on (a part of your body)

◆ **Take off :** to remove a piece of clothing from (a part of your body)

Look at the examples :

- **Put on** your shirt. **Put** your shirt **on**. Take off your shirt.
- **Take** your shirt **off**.
- He **took** off his jeans and **put on** the suit before the train reached Delhi.
- She **took** her nightie **off** and put a sari on before getting off the train.
- Would you **take off** your gloves for clearing? Please **take** them **off**.
- I don't know what dress to **put on**.

■ **Words and expressions connected with fitness**

Suit; sit well; fit; well stitched; finely stitched

Look at the examples :

- This dark suit **sits** very **well** on you. (Sits well = fits very well)
- The blue coloured salwar kurta sits **well** on your slim body.
- The coat **sits badly** across your shoulders. It's **too big** for your.

- These pants **fit** me perfectly; they're neither too big for you.
- The **tailor-made** suit you're wearing doesn't fit you well.
- The skirt she's wearing is beautifully **tailored.** It fits her **well**.
- The top doesn't **fit** your **very well;** but the skirt is all right.
- The **wedding dress** she's (= she has) made is **well-stitched**.
- The shirt with **finely stitched** collars is very expensive.
- This dress looks beautiful but that isn't **well stitched**.
- It's **too narrow** at the bottom

- **To put on (to see if a piece of clothing fits well)**

Here are some examples :

- What a lovely dress! Why don't you try it on, Moni?
- He **tried on** the coat to see if it was **the right size.**
- He went to **the tailor's** to **have/get** his new suit **tried on**.
- It doesn't **fit** me at all. Can I **try on** that one?

Note : the tailor's

- **Words and expressions connected with fitness :**

Close-fitting = not loose, *e.g.*

I don't like clothes **fitting close** to the body.

- **Close-fitting** clothes are uncomfortable. I prefer a **bigger** size.
- **Loose-fitting** = clothes that are **large;** don't fit your body **tightly.**

Example : He was wearing a lungi and a **loose-fitting** skirts.
- **Tightly-fitting** = tightly fitting, *e.g.* She likes **tight-fitting** skirts.

I hate girls roaming the campus in **tightly fitting** jeans.

Also : these pants are a **tight fit** (= fitting tight)
- **Baggy** = baggy clothes are too big; hang loosely on the body, eg.

- Your sweater has gone all **baggy** in the wash
- He was in the **baggy suit**/the pajamas are **baggy** at the knees.
- She was wearing **baggy** trousers.

Look at the following phrases :

(b) Let out = make a piece of clothing wider or loser.

Let down = make a piece of clothing longer

Look at the examples :

- The skirt was **too short;** I asked my tailor to **let** it **out** (= make it larger) a bit.

- Please, **let out** these trousers a bit more; they're **too tight** around the waist.
- You've **grown** so **fat** that you'll have to **let your trousers** out **several inches.**

  (to the tailor) : Will you **let down** these trousers for me?

(c) Tuck in/into = put a piece of clothing inside knickers/pants, etc, *e.g.*

- Your shirt's hanging out, **tuck** it **in**. (= Put it inside your trousers)
- He **tucked** his shirt **into** his shorts/she **tucked** her sari round her waist.

❑❑❑

Unit-38 Clothes, Jewellery and Cosmetics

(वस्त्र, आभूषण और प्रसाधन सामग्री)

Buttons, zip, studs, etc. are small things called fasteners. They are used to fasten (=close) or unfasten clothes. There are some verbs particularly connected with fasteners; some others are connected with dressing and undressing. This unit deals with these devices and their uses in detail.

- **Look at the following words**
  - **Fasten (v)** : to join together the two sides of something, eg : a coat, shirt etc.
  - **Unfasten (v)** : to undo (= untie) something that it tied or wrapped, *e.g.*
    I can't unfasten this button.
  - **Fastener (n)** : a device such as, a button that fastens something, especially a piece of clothing. Some other such devices are : studs, hooks, zips, etc.

The phrase **"fasten up"** means : to **close** something **completely**.

Note : 'up' can be used before or after the object

Look at the examples :

- **Fasten** your coat/**fasten up** your coat/**fasten** your coat **up**.
- He was sitting having a belt **fastened** <u>around</u> him in his car.
- He **fastened up** his pajamas with a narrow piece of string.
- **Unfasten/Undo :** to open, *e.g* - **unfasten/undo** the buttons of your shirt.

- **Buttons as fasteners :**

You **fasten/unfasten** a button or buttons **on** your shirt.

Examples :
- It's very cold outside. **Button** your coat.
- **Button up** your coat. It's very cold outside.
- **Button up** your jeans, you silly! (= Fasten up ...)
- **Button** your jeans **up**.

- **Unbutton (v) :** unfasten buttons on something, *e.g.*
  - The police **unbuttoned** his jacket to make a thorough search.
  - The official at customs asked him to **unbutton** his coat.
  - The principal scolded the boy for loitering **unbuttoned.**

- **Buttoned down collars :** shirts with pointed collars.
Colars of this type are **fastened** to the shirt by **buttons,** *e.g.*
One of the **buttons** of my shirt has **come off**.
Will you please fasten it **up**?

- **Studs :** something like a button used for fastening clothes.
  - **Collar studs/press studs :** fasteners of this kind have two round parts, one of which is pressed into the hollow part of the other.
  - **Cufflink :** cufflinks are small objects.
  These are used for holding together (= fastening) shirt cuffs.
  - **Hook/eye** these are used for fastening clothes, *e.g.*
  The jacket he bought is **hooked** at the back/her blouse is fastened with hooks and **eyes**.
  He **hooks** the waistband onto the eye for keeping his trousers tight.

- **Zip :** a fastener that is used on clothing *e.g.*
  - Can you help me; I can't **zip up** my top.
  - The **zip** on my trousers has broken/he **zipped** his jacket **open**.
  - The **zip** on my trousers has stuck/**zip up** my trousers.
  Unzip : open something by pulling a zip fastner, *e.g.*
  - He **unzipped** the jacket/she **unzipped** her dress, etc.

- **Shoe-laces (जूते के फीते) :** a lace is string or cord used to fasten or tighten shoes.
Examples : She's **lacing** her shoes/**lace up** your shoes.
(**Lace up** = fasten by tying a lace)
he was **tying** the **laces** of his shoes/**ties up** your **laces.**

- **Look at the following words and their uses :**
Sew'stitch/crochet/knit/darn/embroider
Sew (सिलना) : pronounce this word as 'Sou' and Sewed (pt.) as 'soud'.
Sewn (सिला) : is pronounced as 'Soun'.
Sew : stitch; making or repairing clothes, *e.g.*
I'm very good at sewing/she's going to **do** some **sewing** etc.
Sew (on) : attach with needle and thread.
  - She sewed the badge neatly **on** his coat.
  - Can you sew a patch **on** my trousers?

Sew a button (on) : She's **sewing on** buttons/I'm bad at sewing on buttons.
Excuse me! Can you **sew** a button **on** my shirt, please?

Sorry! I'm busy. You must know how to **sew on** buttons.

Sew up : repair/join, eg.

- Can you **sew up** this hole in my coat?
- Could you please **sew up** these two pieces of cloth?

■ **Stitch** (टांका लगाना, सिलाई करना) = moving a needle and thread in band out of cloth, eg.

- She **stitched** the button **on** his shirt/he **stitched** a flower on the table-cloth.
- She put a few **stitches** in the **tear** (= hole) and the frock was as good as new.
- She **stitched** the **tear** at the elbow of his coat.

■ **Crochet** (कसीदाकारी) **:** a small needle with a hook to make clothes, blankets etc, eg. Women were **crocheting** blankets/shawls/monograms in the factory.

Knit (बुनना) **:** making articles of cloting from woolen threads, eg.

She was **knitting** gloves**/a sweater/scarf,** etc.

■ Can you **knit** a sweater for me? Sorry! I don't have time for knitting.

Knit up : She **knitted up** a pair of socks for me.

She wore a cardigan **knitted** in imported wool.

■ **Dran :** to mend a hole by weaving in a piece of clothing, eg.

- She has/she's been **darining** for hours. Can you **darn** my socks?
- I don't have needle for **darning**/this cardigan is full of darns (repairs).

■ **Embroider** (कढ़ाई, कशीदाकारी) **:** to make designs on cloth, eg.

- She's **embroidering** patterns/Can you **embroider** a butterfly on my hankie?
- He has **embroidered** pictures on his shawl/She wore a richly **embroidered** sari.
- The cushions were **embroidered** with flowers.

■ **Uses of 'wear' in everyday speech**

Wear : have (clothes/clothing) on body or part of it.

Also : You wear shoes/specs/jewellery/perfume/fragrance/wig/make up

Look at the examples :

- Children wear school dress. **Wearing** sari is common in India.
- Children with weak eyesight **wear** glasses (= spectacles)
- People **wear** sunglasses to protect their eyes from sunlight.
- Goggles are **worn** to protect eyes from chemicals, wind, water, etc.
- You **wear** gloves **on** your hands/socks **on** the feet inside your shoes.

- Did you notice the **dress** Mrs Tiwari was **wearing** at the party?
- He **wore** a tie round the neck and a **flower in the buttonhole.**
- **She was** wearing **ribbons** in **her hair and slippers** on **her feet.**

Put on/take off (पहनना/उतारना) (verbs of action) :

'Put on' and **'take off'** are used for dressing and undressing, *e.g.*

- I **put on** my clothes, belt, tie and glasses when I go to the office.
- I **take** my clothes **off** before having a bath every morning.
- He **took off** his hat and shoes before entering the temple.
- Wait a minute! I haven't **put on** my clothes yet.

Wearing jewellery : (गहना पहनना)

Women '**wear**' jewellery such as, necklace, bracelet, gold bangles, earrings, nose pin, clipon, rings, studs, etc. **on** different parts of their body; rich women '**wear**' precious stones, *e.g.* Diamond, pearl necklace, etc. as body decorations.

Look at the examples :

Fasten (to) – women **fasten** earrings **to** theirs ears.

Wear (on/in) – people **wear** ornaments **on** different parts of their body, *e.g.*

Mr Yogi **wears** an auspicious ring **on** his left hand finger and a diamond studded platinum ring **on** his right hand finger. Mrs Yogi **wore** a large nose ring and the wedding ring **on** her right hand finger. On occasions she **wears** hoop/earrings and studs **in** her ears. She likes to **wear** nose pin as well.

Wear nose pin as well.

Wear (on/around) – Most women **wear** gold bangles **around** their wrists and bracelets **on/around** their arms. Women who are rich **wear** gold/ pearls necklace **around** their neck.

Put on/take off (पहनना/उतारना)(verbs of action) :

Put on : to have or place a piece of jewellery on/over a part of the body.

Take off : to remove something from its place, eg. He **took off** his ring.

Look at these examples :

- I'd rather **put on** my hoop earrings and the diamond necklace.
- It's a bad women to **take off** one's wedding ring. **Put** it **on** your finger.
  Note : 'bad women' is a sign of bad happening in the future.
- She **took** her jewellery **off** before going out/Why don't you **put on** your anklets?

- She **puts on** her best jewellery and matching bangles on especial occasions.

▪ People 'wear' perfume like jewellery and clothing

(लोग कपड़े और आभूषणों की तरह इत्र का इस्तेमाल करते हैं)

Look at the examples :

- What perfume would you like to wear? I'd like to wear French perfume.
- Only the rich can afford to **wear** expensive perfumes and fragrances.
- She often **wears** musk when going to the dance hall.
- I never like **wearing** perfumes and fragrances.

▪ 'Wearing' make up (= cosmetics)

'Wearing' make up means : to have it on the face or some part of your body.

Men **Wear** make-up to improve their appearance and women to look more attractive.

Put on make up (= apply make up)

Look at the examples :

- She's so crazy that she won't step out without **making up**.
- On special occasions she **wears** heavy **make-up**.
- The newly wedding girl **wore** thick lipstick and mascara/she likes to **put on** expensive **make-up**.
- Television artists **put on** thick **make-up** before appearing on the screen.

Short-dialogue :

Moni : Which colour do you wear?
Asha : Not too bright.
Moni : put on this one, it's all suit you.

▪ Talking about artificial/natural hair

(कृत्रिम/प्राकृतिक बालों के बारे में बातचीत)

People **wear** artificial hair (= wig) and moustache to hide their appearance.

He was **wearing** a black **wig** over his hair/she **wore** a **wig** on the head.

He **put on** a thing beard and black moustache before coming on the stage.

For natural hair, say :

The tall man **wore** a beard and moustache / He had a **beard** and moustache.

Who's that man **wearing** curly hair and white moustache?

Unit-39

Switches and Buttons
(स्विच और बटन)

Switches and buttons are control device which regulate machines, electricity and object like, radio, television, etc. They are part of our routine tasks and activities; we make use of them frequently for various purposes. In this unit, some common verbs are phrases relating to the functioning of these devices have been discussed at length.

(a) Hold down (दबाए रखना) (= keep down) :

Please **hold down** the shift key and press 'Y'.

Turn (up/down) : to increase or reduce the amount of heat, *e.g :*

It's very cold; will you **turn up** the heating, please?

Note : 'heating' is a system for making a building warm.

(b) Push (दबाना/धक्का देना) : press, *e.g.*

- He **pushed** the buttons to start/stop the engine.
- Will you **push** that lever to the machine, please?
- **Push** this button if you want to fire the gun.

(c) Turn (on/off) :

When you **tun on** the switch or knob of something, *e.g :* Light/radio/television/tape/gas/electricity, etc. it starts working.

When you **turn** it **off,** you stop it working.

Look at the examples :

- Push the left button to **turn** the lights **on.**
- She **turned** the television **on.** (- Switched on)
- He **turned on** the street lights/**turn off** the lights, please.
- Will you **turn off** the tape? (= stop the flow of water)

(d) Switch on (चालू करना) : turn on

You **switch on** to connect a power supply/an appliance, *e.g.*

It's getting dark; **switch on** the lights, please. (= turn on the lights, please)

(d) Switch off (बंद करना) : turn off. (You switch off to stop the supply of electricity)

Here are some examples :

- Don't forget to **switch off** (= turn off) before you leave the house.
- You must **switch off** (= turn off) **at** the mains when you're at work (= working).
- I **switched off** (= turned off) the lights and got into bed.

Note : switch **on/off** and turn **on/off** can be used to **connect/disconnect** appliances such as : heater/washing machine/grinder/supply (of water, gas and electricity).

(f) Plug (in/into) : to push a plug in/into an electric socket.

Look at the examples :

- Computers can be **plugged into** TV sets/he plugged the television **into** the wall socket.
- She **plugged** the lamp **into** its socket; **plug in** (connect) and **turn** the tape **on**.
- I think he hasn't **plugged in** the antenna right. **Plug in** the earphones, please.

Plug (n) : a two or three pin plug, *e.g.*

- Would you **put** the plug **into** the socket?/**Push in** the plug before **turning on** the TV.
- She **pushed/inserted** the plug **into** the socket.
- **Turn** the television **off** at the plug.

(g) Put on : switch on (= connect a power supply), *e.g.*

- Will you **put on** the lights/**put** the lights **on**, please.
- Will you **put** the lights **on?** It's getting dark.

Put out : switch off (= stop working/disconnect), *e.g.*

- He put out the light.
- She **put** the light **out** and closed the door.
- Could you **put** the lights **out?**
- He undressed and **put out** the light.

■ **Knob** (n) : a control button

Turn (v) : to move, *e.g.*

- He oiled the **knob** and **turned** it several times.
- He turned the **knob** to open the box/Can you **turn** the **knob**?
- He **turned** the **knob** to increase/adjust the volume.

Handle (n) a lever used for opening/closing a door, *e.g.*

- I **turned** the **handle** but the door didn't open.

- He **turned** the **handle** so hard that it came off.
- **Turn** its **handle** to the right if you want to start the engine.

■ **Tap** (n) : a device to control the flow of water, *e.g.*
Don't leave the tap running.

Here are some examples :

- Who's (= who has) left the **tap** running? Please, **turn** it **off**.
- I can hear water running from a **tap.** Would someone **tun** it **off, please?**
- I think you've left the bathroom **tap on**. Will you **turn it** off?
- It's no use **turning** the **tap on;** it's running dry.

❑❑❑

Unit-40 Types of Light
(प्रकाश के प्रकार)

People use electricity for various purposes in everyday life. it provides heat and light, drives machines, operates computers, etc. This energy is produced in power station. Other sources of energy are : fire which generates hot bright flames and the sun that gives out rays of light. The present unit deals with words and phrases connected with electricity, electric light and extra source of energy.

The Electric Light (बिजली की रोशनी)

When an electric bulb **fuses,** it stops burning and you say :
The **light** isn't working/the bulb has **fused**/please, bring a new bulb.
If a **fuse** occurs **at the mains** (= place of the main supply of electricity)
You say : I think the **fuse** has **blown/gone** at the mains.
The high voltage has **fused** all the lights.
Has the **fuse** blown? / Call someone to **mend** the **fuse,** please.

- **Go out** (गुल होना, बुझ जाना) (= stop burning/shining)

In case of '**power cut**' **or** '**power failure**' the supply is interrupted.
Electric bulbs stop shining; it gets dark all around and you say :
'The **lights** have **gone out**'.

Look at these examples :

- The light (= electricity) **went out** and we were left in the dark.
- The lights in our city usually **go out** at peak hours.
- "When did the light **go out?**" asked he.
- I think it **went out** quite early this morning.
- The lights would **go out** if it rained heavily.
- What would you do if the lights **went out**?

- **Go off** (बंद हो जाना) **:** to stop operating/working

Look at the examples :

- In the storm the lights flickered and suddenly **went off**.
- Lights usually **go off/out** for hours during load shedding.
- The electricity stopped (= **went off**) due to short-circuit.

- We were watching a TV serial when the light **went off.**
- I couldn't study as the light **went off** in my room.

- **Come on :** start operating again, *e.g. :*
  - The light has come on (= started working)
  - It's **getting** dark and the lights **at** the poles haven't **come on** yet.
  - The light has **gone out** and won't **come on** unit six o'clock.
  - The light **went off** suddenly and didn't **come on** for hours.
  - There was no light all day; it **came on** only after midnight.
  - They can't get on with their work until lights **come on.**
  - When did the lights **come on** last night.

Extra Source of Light (प्रकाश के अतिरिक्त साधन)

- **Battery :** a device that produces electricity.

  Look at the examples :
  - The **front lights** of your car aren't working.
  - The battery's **gone**, I think. (= The battery has gone .....)
  - The battery is dead. (= It's gone). You need a new one.
  - The battery needs recharging the front/side **lights** are dim.

- **Fire :** this is another source of light.

  Light (v) : to make something start burning, *e.g.* : a fire/candle/lamp.

  Verb forms : Light lighted/lit (pt.), lighted/lit. (pp)

  Note : The usual pt. and pp form of light is **'lit'**.

  The word 'lighted' is generally used before a noun.

  Look at the examples :
  - It was dark inside; so she **lit** a match/an oil lamp/a fire.
  - He **lit** a fire/Monika put the **lighted** match to the papers.
  - They **lighted** a large fire/he was holding a **lighted** candle.
  - The fire was still **blazing** (= burning), **lighting up** the sky.
  - He **lit** a cigarette/**lit up** small fires here and there.

- **Phrases connected with fire**
  - **Set fire to :** cause something to burn, damage or destroy, *e.g. :* The crowd **set** fire to the building (= they **set** the building **on fire**)
  - **Catch fire :** start burning (by accident) The building **caught fire**/the building was **on fire** (= burning)
  - **Put out :** stop burning or shining, eg. **Put out** all the lights, please.

Here are some more examples :

- He **lighted** a fire/she **put out** the fire/please **light** a lamp/candle.
- He **lighted** the cigarette/match. Please **put out** the cigarette/match.

Note : Match (a short think stick)/**Match-box** (matches are sold in it).

◆ **Blow out (बुझ जाना) :** to stop burning (with a puff of air), *e.g.* :
A flame, fire, light, candle, lamp, etc ....

Look at the examples :

- She **blew out** the candle. (= She putted out the candle)
- She **blew** the candle **out**. (= She putted the candle out)
- A sudden rush of wind **blew out** the flickering light.
- He **blew out** the flame of his lighter.

◆ **Go out :** stop burning (with a puff of air), *e.g.* :

- The candle **went out** when I was writing a letter. (= stopped burning)
- He **lit** a **fire** to keep the room warm but it **went out** before midnight.
- Excuse me! Have you got **'a light'**, please? My cigarette's **gone out.**

Note : 'a light' is a match (= cigarette lighter) to light a cigrette.

■ **Other source of light (प्रकाश के अन्य स्रोत)**

Examples :

- The sun **shines; it gives out rays** of light.
- White hot coal on a fire glows. Stars **shine** (twinkle/glimmer)
- Your torch gives out a **beam** = (= ray) of light.
- A camera gives a **flash** of light/diamond necklace **sparkles.**
- Jewellery **glitters** (= give off many small **flashes** of light)

❑❑❑

Unit-41 Musical Instruments and Devices

(संगीत वाद्ययंत्र और उपकरण)

This unit deals with some of the words and expressions most commonly used in the context of music and musical instruments. It also presents the vocabulary for talking about electronic devices such as, radio and television which are essential part of modern entertainment. To being with, let's discuss about the word 'play' and it's different uses.

- **Play** (v) : to perform a piece of music on a musical instrument.

  Look at the examples :

  - He **plays** the harmonium/she **plays** the sitar and her sister **plays** the flute.
  - She was **playing** the dholak while I was **playing** the majeera at the kirtan.
  - I played the guitar **at** the concert; my son accompanied me **at** the tabla.
  - It took me five years **to play** the piano perfectly/Can you **play** the violin?
  - How long have you been **playing** the drums?/**playing** the flute difficult.

  Note : 'the' is used with musical instrument.

Playing a Tune (धुन बजाना)

Note : a 'tune' is a series of musical notes.

Look at the examples

- The orchestra was **playing** the popular **tune** of a well-known song.
- can **play** any **tune** on the guitar with perfect ease and confidence.
- I hear the clarinet **playing** Bhairvi on the radio every morning.
- What **tune** are you going to **play** now?

- **Playing Ragas/notes :** ('Notes' are musical sounds)

  Raga : a traditional Indian pattern of notes.

  Examples :

  - We heard him **play** the raga 'Yaman' on the violin.
  - He played a few notes on the piano; his performance was superb.

Strike (= play) :

- If you **Strike** a note/cord on the sitar and the audience clapped loudly.
- He **struck** a few notes on the sitar and the audience clapped loudly.

Player : performer of an instrument, eg. He's a famous sitar **player**.
The man accompanying him at the tabla is an ordinary player.

■ Playing electronic musical devices (विद्युत वाद्ययंत्र बजाना)

'Play' also means : to produce sounds or pictures.

For example :

- You **play** a device such as, a tape (for recording). If a CD or cassette.
- **Plays**, or if you **play** it, it produces sound or music.
- You **play** music by using stereo (a machine for playing records).

■ Play back (phr v) :

Used to show (something) again that you have recorded.

Examples :

- I'd like (= I want) to watch the picture you've recorded.
- Will you **play** the film **back?** (= Will you replay the film?)

Playback (n) : replay, *e.g. :*

- Let's have a **playback** of the President's speech we heard last night.
- Will you press the **playback** button? I wish to listen to the song you've recorded.

Electronic Devices (विद्युत उपकरण)

Connected words and phrases

- ◆ **Insert/turn on :**
  Will you turn the record **off**, please? The noise is giving me a headache.
- ◆ **Turn down :** to reduce the sound, eg.
  Can you **turn** the volume **down** a bit on the stereo?
- ◆ **Put into :** insert, eg.
  - **Put** this cassette **into** the VCP/VCR and turn it on.
  - Will you **put** the CD **into** the computer, please?
- ◆ **Put on/listen (to) :**
  Put the record **on** the record player and **turn** it **on**.
  He invited me to **listen to** his new CD/I'm listening to the music.
  Don't say :
  Hear/hearing the music, cassette, etc.

Say : listen/listening (to) the music, cassette etc.

Note : 'hear' is not normally use in the continuous form.

- **Dance (to) :**

  Say : I **played** the record and everyone **danced** to the music.

  They **danced** to the orchestra that was **playing** a famous tune.

Radio and television (रेडियो और टेलीविजन)

Switch (on/off); **turn** (on/off)

These phrase are used to mean : to operate/stop a device.

Look at the examples :

- Would you **turn** the radio **off**? The children are studying.
- She **turned** the television **on** to watch her favourite programme.

Playing the radio

Play : to produce sounds/music (from), *e.g.*

- Will you **play** the radio?/she **plays** her radio all day long.
- He's (= he has) been **playing** the radio for two hours.
- 'Soft music was **playing** and the lights were low.'

Note : use definite article 'the' with radio, *e.g.*

- When I came in, **he was** listening to **the** radio.
- Did you listen to the broadcast **on** the radio.

Listen (to) : (सुनना)

- He was **listening to** his favourite programme **on** the radio.
- He asked me which radio station I mostly **listen to**.
- She **put** the radio **on** to **listen to** the news.
- I don't much **listen to** the radio.

  Note : When you 'hear' something attentively, you **listen to** it.

  '**Hear**' is used in a general sense, eg. I **heard** some old songs.

  I **heard** them talking, but didn't **listen to** what they were talking about.

  Note : 'to' is used when an object follows listen (eg. listen to the song)

On/over the radio : (रेडियो पर)

Look at the following examples :

- She **heard** this news **on** the radio.
- The match will be relayed **live** (real) **on** all radio station.
- I **heard** an interesting programme **on** the radio last night.

- Did you **hear** his speech **on** the radio this morning?
- His talk on foreign policy **over** the radio (= using 'radio')

■ How to use the phrase 'tune in' :

Tune in (to) – to set a radio/television to a particular station, *e.g.*

- I **tuned** my radio **to** the BBC World Service.
- **Tune in to** this station, please/she **tuned in to** (listen to) "News at Night".
- In the Hall were two television sets, each **tuned to** a different station.
- Please don't forget to **tune in** next Friday at the same time, Good Night!

■ Volume : turn up/down, *e.g.*

- It's too loud. Can you **turn** the volume **down,** please?
- I can't **hear** what it is **playing**. Can you turn the sound up?

■ Television

Examples : I've got a 15-inch colour TV. (**Don't say :** coloured)
What's on television this evening? (= Going to broadcast on ....)
Note : 'broadcast' as a verb form remains the same in all tenses.
But : in Am English its pt and pp. is 'broadcasted.'
Say : I'm **watching** TV/she's **watching** a film **on** television.
Do you **watch** a lot of television?/Will you **switch on** TV, please?
I'd like to **watch** my favourite serial.
Some of the old films will be **shown on** television this week.
The radio was **on**/the television was **on** (= continuing)

■ Watch (देखना) (v) : used to express some kind of movement/motion.

It shows that something is 'happening' or going to happen, *e.g.*
I'm **watching** the game/he's **watching** the film.
Remember ; you **'watch'** an activity (that needs your attention).
But : you **'see'** a thing by chance, without being conscious of it.
Generally 'See' is not used in the continuous form, *e.g.*
Wrong : I'm <u>seeing</u> somebody coming.
Right : I **can** see somebody's coming.
'See' can be used with 'can' or 'could', for example :
She couldn't **see** me in the crowd.

Note : You **'watch'** television, etc.
But, **see** 'public performances' of **plays** and films.

Look at the examples :

- Did you **watch** 'Carina' last night" (A TV serial)
- Have you **seen** Mughal-e-Azam in its new form? (A film)
- We **saw** 'Meghdoot' **at** an open air **theatre** in Mumbai last year. (A play)

- **Channel :** a television station, *e.g.* : a sports channel/music channel, etc.

Here are some examples :

- The oath taking ceremony will be telecast/shown broadcast **on** all the **channels**.
- You can **watch** the **live** telecast of the Olympic Games **on** the sports **channel**.
- The national **channel** will **televise** (= broadcast) the film Mughal-e-Azam tonight.
- I **turned on** TV to **watch** the news **on channel** two.
- Will you **switch** on to some other channel, please? I want to **see** a film.

- **Talking about 'VDO'**

Video is a machine that **plays** video tapes **on** a television set.
It also **records** television programmes **onto** a video cassette. (Onto = on)

Learn these words and phrases :

- **Turn on/off :**
  - The teacher **turned** the video **on** to teach English to his students.
  - You should **turn off** the video after showing the film.
- **Play/watch :**
  - A video tape/cassette can be **played** and **watched** on a TV set.
  - He was **playing** the video cassette of his marriage?
- **Full up :** filled completely, *e.g.*

  This video is **full up**. Have you got any blank ones?

Video (v) : to record a TV programme/film/wedding etc. on a video tape, *e.g.*

It's a fashion now to 'Video' a wedding/Can you **video** this documentary?

(**Video a wedding :** record a wedding onto videotape)

Blank Video; on video

Examples :

Have you got a **blank video**?/this film is now available **on video** as well.

VCR : (Video cassette recorder)

A **VCR** is a machine that can record sounds and pictures from a television **onto** a tape.

Video cassettes can also be played **on** it.

Unit-42

Weight and Measures

(वजन और माप)

'Measurement' refers to size, weight, distance, etc. You measure things in your house, at school and other places using various units of measurement. Machines make thousands of measurements everyday. The present unit deals with different ways of asking and answering questions connected with measurement.

Measuring weight (वजन मापना)

Look at these words : weights, weighing, weighed

Here are some examples :

Informal	**Formal**
How much does she weigh?	(= What's her weight?)
She weighs seventy kilos.	(= her weight is seventy kilos)
How much did it weigh?	(= What was the weight of it?)
It weighed 30 kilograms.	(= its weight was 30 kilograms)
How much do you weigh?	(= What's your weight?)
I **weigh** 68 kilograms.	(= My weight is 68 kilograms)

Look at these examples:

I'm the **same** weight **as** I was 20.	(Don't say : 20 years old)
How heavy is this bag?	(= What's the weight of this bag?)
This bag weighs 10 kg.	(= It's ten kilos in weight)
It **weighs** a little less.	(= a bit less) than ten kg.

- **Put on weight** (= become heavier)

  Examples : He **weighed** 65 kilos a few months ago.

  He **weighs** seventy kilos now. he's heavier than before.

  How much has he gained?

  He's (= he has) gained (= added) five kilos.

  How much does Amit weigh? He weights 75 kilos.

  He's (= he has) **put on** much weight.

  He's (= he has) **put on** over a kilo in three months.

- **Give short measure :** give less amount/weight

  The shopkeeper cheats you if he gives you short measure.

Look at the examples :

- The potatoes **weighed** on the scales were **short in measure**.
- He was fined for **giving short measure** (= less amount)
- I don't go to that shop. They **give short measure**.
- He's a cheater. he **gives short measure**.

Measuring height (ऊँचाई मापना)

When you say :

"How tall are you?" it means : **"What's your height?"**

The answer can be : I'm five feet seven (inches)

(Or) : I'm five foot seven. (informal)

Questions and Answers

Q. : How tall are you?
Ans : I'm only six feet tall.
Q. : How tall is Amit?
Ans : He's 5 feet 6".
Q. : How tall is Soni?
Ans : She's 5 feet 3", and Sonia? She's (of) the same height. (= Both are the same height). But, I'm taller of the two.

Mountains/buildings : (questions and answers)

Q. : How high is the Empire State Building? **(= What's the height of ....?)**
Ans : **It is/It's** 1,250 feet above the ground. **How high is** Everest? It's about 29,00 feet.

Tall/high (लम्बाई/ऊँचाई)

Remember : 'High' refers to distance upwards, *e.g.*

- The 'Buland Darwaja' is **the highest** gateway in India.
- Everest is **the highest** mountain in the world.

Tall : this is generally used of people.

But : a tree is **'tall'** if it has a greater than average height.

Examples :

- **'Palm'** and **'bamboo'** trees are **tall** (not high)
- **'Skyscrapers'** with **several storeys** are **tall** buildings.
- The **'Kutub Minaret'** in Delhi is **the tallest** tower in India.
- A **flagpole**, and a **church spire** are **tall** objects.

- **Distance** (दूरी)

Asking and answering questions :

Q. : **How far is it from London to Paris?**
Ans : It is/It's 215 miles.
Q. : How far is it from Agra to Delhi?
Ans : It is/It's three hundred kilometres.
Q. : How far is it from here to the railway station?
Ans : it's about two kilometers.
Q. : **Is it far from here to Connaught Place?**
Ans : Yes. It's 10 kilometres from here.
Q. : Is it far from here to the airport?
Ans : **Yes. It's a (very) long way**.
It's only **a short distance** from here. (= It's only **a short way** from here).
(Or) No, I it isn't **far**/it's **very near**/it's only ½ **a kilometre** from here
It's only **a ten minutes' walk/ride** from here.

- **Dimensions** (आयाम, लंबाई-चौड़ाई) **:** size (length, width and height)

Area : (length × width)
When someone asks about the area of your room, you say :
"It is/Its twelve feet by fifteen feet" (12 × 15) = 180 sq. feet.
Similarly : A room ten feet by ten feet (10 0215 10) is **ten feet square**
Meaning : 100 square feet (**'foot'** can be used informally), eg :
My sitting room is about twelve foot by fifteen, etc.

- **Question and answers :**

Q. : How long is this room?
Ans : It's twelve feet (long). Or : It's twelve feet **in length**.
Q. : How long is your table?
Ans : It's five feet three (inches)
It's five feet three **in length**.
Q. : **How high is it?** It's three and a quarter feet (high)
Ans : It's three and a quarter feet **in height**.
Q. : **How wide is it?** It's nine and a half feet wide.
Ans : It's nine and a half feet in width.

- **How deep is ....?**

Look at the examples :

How deep is your swimming pool? it's not **deep** enough.
It's 8 feet deep. (= it's 8 feet **in depth**)
How deep did you dive? I dived 6 feet **into** the swimming pool.

Unit-43 Some/Any/No/None

(कुछ/कोई/नहीं/कुछ भी नहीं)

- **Some/any** (कुछ/कोई भी)

Some : shows an amount or number of (something)

'Some' and 'any' are the most frequently used words in everyday speech. 'Some' refers to an amount or number and has nothing to do with how large or small the quantity or number is. It is used mainly in statements rather than questions.

- **'Some' is the plural of a/an**

Look at examples :

- There is a chair in the room. There are **some** chairs in the room.
- There's a picture in my room. There are **some** pictures in the hall.
- There's **an** egg in the basket. There are **some** eggs in the fridge.
- I want a post card and **some** stamps. She wants **some** envelopes.
- Manisha wants **a** piece of cake and **some** biscuits.

- **'Some' refers to a certain quantity** (not clearly started)

Here are some examples :

- There's **some** bread in the fridge. I've bought **some** sugar.
- She has/she's got **some** money. She wants to buy **some** ice cream.
- He is/he's hungry. You must give him **some** food to eat.
- I've made **some** nice coffee. Please give me **some**.

- **Don't say :** There are not <u>some</u> chairs. **Say :** There aren't **any** chairs.

Don't say : Are there <u>some</u> chairs? **Say :** Are there <u>any</u> chairs?

Remember : 'some' is **replaced** by **'any'** in **negatives** and **questions**.

Look at these examples :

- There are **some** boys in the class. There aren't **any** boys in the class.
- Are there **any** boys in the class? ('Any' expresses doubt here).
- I bought **some** apples. I didn't buy **any** apples. Did you **buy** any apples?
- I've got **some** money. I haven't (got) **any** money. Have you got **any** money?
- There's **some** tea in the kettle. There isn't **any** tea in the kettle.
- Is there **any** tea in the kettle? Isn't there **any** tea in the kettle.
- Yes, there is **some**. Sorry! There isn't **any**.

Consider the following :

- **Some** people are standing over there. Do you know **any** of them?
- Is there **any** whisky in the bottle? I'm sorry there isn't **any**.
- Is there **any more** tea in the pot? I think there isn't **any**.
- Is there **any more** soup? Sorry, there isn't **any** left.
- Is there **any** tea, Mum? Sorry, there isn't **any**.

■ **'Some' in questions usually expects a positive answer.**

Look at the examples :

- Have you got **some** money? (Perhaps he's got enough)
- Can I have **some** sugar, please? (Possibly there's a plenty of it)

Look at these, too :

- Aren't there **some more** chairs? (Perhaps there are)
- Are there **any more** chairs? (The answer seems uncertain)

■ **'Some' can be used in offer and requests,** *e.g.* :

- Will you have **some** tea? Would you like **some** coffee?
- Would you like **some** cake? Do you want **some** sugar?
- Wouldn't you like **some more** coffee? **A little**, thank you.
- Have some tea? **No. Thanks.** Can I have **some** ice cream.
- Shall I bring you **some** pastry?

■ **Compounds :**

Somebody/someone = some person (male of female)
Note : there is no difference in meaning of these words.

Look at the examples :

There's **somebody** at the door.	There's **someone** at the door.
There isn't **anybody** at the door.	There isn't **anyone** at the door.
Is there **anybody** at the door?	Is there **anyone** at the door.

Anyone (कोई भी) : any person (in a group), no matter who that person is.
Anybody (कोई भी) : anyone; any person, eg.

- Anyone/anybody will tell you where the station is.
- Has anyone/anybody seen my ball pen and the note book?
- Is anyone here? Is there anybody who knows the answer?

No-one (कोई नहीं) (Also : No one). **Nobody :** not anyone/no person at all, *e.g. :*
There was <u>no one</u> in the class/<u>nobody</u> answered my question.

Something (कुछ, कोई चीज) = an object, etc; (a contrast to nothing) *e.g.* : There's something in his pocket/I want to tell you something.

Nothing (कुछ नहीं) = not anything, eg. There's nothing in his pocket.

Anything (कुछ भी नहीं) = no matter what, eg. Has anything happened. Come to me if you want anything.

- **"No" :** (More emphatic)

  "Not any" (कोई भी नहीं) (normally used in conversation)

  Look at these examples :

  - She hasn't put **any** salt in the meat. She has put **no** salt in the meat.
  - There is**n't any** sugar in the coffee. There is **no** sugar in the coffee.
  - There aren't any buses after 9 pm. There are **no** buses after 9 pm.

- **None (कोई भी नहीं)** = not any ('none' is more emphatic than 'not any')

  Look at the following examples :

There's **no** sugar	There is**n't any** sugar.	There's **none**.
There are **no** letters.	There aren**'t any** letters.	There are **none**.
he has **no** apples.	He hasn**'t any** apples.	He has **none**.

- **None of (कोई नहीं)** = not any of

  Note : None of usually takes a plural verb in ordinary Spoken English, *e.g. :*

  - None of us **are** ready yet.
  - None of my friends **live** here/none of those cars **are** mine.

  But : in formal writing a **singular** verb is used, for example :

  - None of those people **is** interested in your project.
  - None of his parents **was** present/none of them **has** enough money.

  Note : When you are referring to an amount/quantity, use a '**singular**' verb.

  Example : None of the food **was** wasted **at** the dinner party.

❑❑❑

Unit-44 Expressing Quantity (I)

(मात्रा व्यक्त करना)

Quantity (मात्रा)

A 'quantity' is an amount or number of something that can be measured of counted. The present unit is connected with words and expressions like, many, much, a lot of, etc. that answer questions such as : How much?/How many?

- **Look at these words : Much/Many** (बहुत/अनेक)

Much : expresses a large amount or quantity of something and is most often used in negative sentences and questions. In affirmative sentences its use is limited.

Look at the examples :

- He drinks too **much**/I wasn**'t much** surprised at the news.
- I don't earn **much** money/there isn't traffic today.
- **Not much** is happening in our college these days.
- **How much** money did he spend on gambling at cards?
- **How much** sugar do you take in your tea?/**much of** the city was destroyed/**much of** the food was wasted.
- **Much** of the recent trouble if from outside.

  Note : of can be used after 'much'.

- **Many** (अनेक) **:** a large number (of)

'Many' is also used in questions and negative sentences. In simple sentences its use is quite formal. Expressions like, a lot of/lots of/a large number (of) plenty (of) are more common than 'much' and 'many' in everyday speech

Look at the following examples :

◆ **Not many** (= only a few)

There weren**'t many** people in the hall**/not many** people have heard his name/I haven't invited **many** people to my birthday party/**How many** brothers and sisters do you have? **Not many** people knew of his past life **Many of** us are part time workers here. **A great many** (= a very large number of) young men died in the Kargil war/**Many a man** (= many men suffered terrible during the partition of India/this has happened **many a time** (= many times) but nobody bothers.

Note : 'many a man' means : 'many times one man'.

- **As/too/so**

The use of as, too, and so is quite normal with 'many'.

Look at the examples :

- Ask them to eat **as** many **as** they want to.
- You've put **too many** books on this shelf.
- **So many** people attended the function.

- **More/Most** (अधिक/सबसे अधिक, अधिकांश)

These are comparative and superlative degrees of 'many'.

Here are some examples :

- This year's maths paper was **more** difficult than last year's.
- His clever salesmanship brings him **more** customers.
- Not only these, but **many more** houses are needed for the poor.
- Lots of students have got US visa and **many more** are still waiting.
- We're expecting **many more** jobs for young men in near future.
- **More** and **more** people are getting interested in buying cell phones.
- **Most** people now understand that smoking is injurious to health.
- **Most** of the working women in this bank are south Indians.
- **Most** Indians who have settled abroad don't want to return home.

- **These phrases are commonly used in every day speech**

A number of; a lot of; a great deal of; plenty of

Lot(s) of : a large amount or number (of)

Look at these examples :

- **A number of** people came to see the exhibition/lots of people drive too fast.
  - I've got **a lot of** friends/he's got **lots of money,** time and energy to waste.
  - I've got **a lot of** work to do/he's wasted a **great deal of** money in gambling.
- **Plenty (of) :** more than is needed.
  - We've got **plenty of** food to eat/she's got **plenty of** time.
  - There are a **plenty of** eggs and **plenty of** milk.

Note : 'quite' and 'rather' can be used before a lot of (Not 'lots of').

For examples :

- When she drank she created **quite a** lot of trouble in the bar.
- The change in the government policy has affected **rather** a lot of people.

▪ Look at the following expressions :

So much; so much as; very much; too much; as much as; make much of, Much the same; not much; a much discussed question; **much to my surprise; Not much good at; a much debated subject.**

Look at the examples :

- It isn't good for your health to eat **so much** salt.
- Life is most unsafe these days because of **so much** violence.
- Thank you **very much/**thank you **so much** for this lovely present.
- They're not **so much** friends **as** lovers. Don't eat **too much** for you now!
- It's **too much** of your dad to invite his friends to dinner everyday.
- it's **as much** your responsibility **as** mine/she is **as much** a friend to me **as** my wife.
- You can take **as much as** you like/I expected **as much** you expected.

Make much of = understand, *e.g.*

I couldn't **make much of** that lecture/their houses are **much the same.** (= Similar)

Is there any tea left? **Not much**/Do you enjoy watching TV? Not much.

Who are forming the government **at** the centre is **a much discussed questions**.

'Reservation' is **a much debated subject** in this country.

Much to my surprise the principal considered my application for admission.

I'm **not much good at** singing.

(a) **'Much'** can be used before adjective, *e.g. :*
This hotel is **much** expensive.
Your culture is **much** different from ours.

(b) **'Much'** can be used before adjectives in the –er form, *e.g.*
It's much cheaper/much bigger/much longer/much better.

(c) **'Much'** can also be used before certain past participles, *e.g.*
She's **much** tried/**much** admired/**much** interested, *etc.*

▪ **'Much'** can be used with comparatives to mean 'a lot.'

Look at the examples :

- It's getting **much colder**/he's **much older** than me.
- She's **much better** now/you must work **much harder**.
- His condition is **much worse** than expected.

- **More (comparative)**

This indicates a large amount, quality, degree, etc.

Look at the examples :

- He's spending **more** time than usual for his final exams.
- He asked them for **more** and **more** money to finish the task quickly.
- I became **more** and **more** intimate with her during my stay in London.
- This problem seems **much more** difficult to solve (= a lot more difficult)
- Is there **any more** cooffee? Sorry, there isn't any left.
- His illness is **much more** serious (= far more/a lot more serious)
- The employers don't want quality work **any more**.
- We don't expect **any more** demand from them.
- Don't worry! I've got **more** than enough money.

- **Most (superlative) :**

Indicates greatest in quantity; nearly all

Note : used in front of adjective and adverb.

Look at the examples :

- He's one of my **most** intimate friends/it was the **most** boring film.
- Tajmahal is one of the **most** beautiful buildings in the world.
- I've eaten **most** of the salad/this is the **most** expensive shop.
- He spends **most** of his time gossiping with his friends.
- He spends **most** of his time gossiping with his friends.
  Most of the left over food was thrown away.
  left over = remaining; unused.

❑❑❑

Unit-45 Expressing Quantity (II)

(मात्रा व्यक्त करना)

Few/Fewer/Fewest

- **Few :** used in a negative sense meaning : 'hardly any'.
  It refers to a small number of people or things and often used after 'very'.

  Look at the examples :
  - I have **few** friends. (= not many)
  - **Few** people can speak Sanskrit perfectly.
  - People suffer but **few** complain.
  - **very few** people can afford to buy luxury cars.
  - There are only **few** options open to you.
  - I have **very few** chocolates left.
  - **Very few** people were lucky to survive the accident.
  - **Very** few reached the summit, the rest perished (= died)

- **'A few'** refers to more than 'few' but not a large number.
  It is used in a positive sense and is equal to 'some' (= a small number)

  Here are some examples :
  - We're going away for **a few** days/the police asked him **a few** questions.
  - I have **a few** friends and we meet quite often (= many times)
  - He's asking me for **a few** more chocolates/give him quite **a few**, please.
  - How many cakes do you want?/**Oh, just** a few, please.
  - There are **a few** days left before we leave for home.

- **'The few'** refers to a small number considered as separate from the majority, *e.g.*
  The few who were awarded gold medals were sitting in the front row.
  The few (= not many) attended the function and they too left early.
  Only **the few** were invited for the final interview.

- **Fewer/the fewest**
  These are the comparative and superlative forms of 'few'
  Look at the examples :
  - **Very few** people become millionaires and **fewer** multi-millionaires.

- I tried to contact him on the phone **no fewer than** ten times.
- **No fewer than** fifty people attended the meeting.
- Fewer people listen to the radio now **than** before.

■ **Little/a little :** these are used with uncountable nouns.

Little suggests a negative idea – 'not much'; 'hardly any'.

It is often used after 'very'.

Look at the examples :

- I get **little** time for reading/she's got **little** patience.
- He has **very little** hope of winning the race.
- They tried their best but made **little** progress.
- **A little :** a small quantity (of) [compare with 'some']

Look at the examples

- Give me **a little** (= a bit of) time to think about it.
- Have you got **any** money? Yes, **a little**.
- How much sauce do you want? Just **a little**, please.
- He knows **a little** French but **a lot of** English.

■ Less/Least

Less : is used with words expressing quantity

'Less' is used with words expressing quantity or amount for example : less food/less butter/less money etc.

Here are some examples :

- I have **less** money than you/ I want **more** work and less talk. He got **much less** than I expected /it costs **less** than Rs. 5-/-.
- Spend **less** and save **more** for a rainy day (= for the future)
- Drink **more** milk and eat **less** chocolate.
- He took the medicine in **less** quantity.
- He died in **less** than three weeks.

■ **Least :** smallest in size/amount, etc.

Look at the examples

- She has **little** money, you have **less** than her and I have the **least**.
- **The least** said the better; the best is to keep silence.
- I believe in doing the things that cost **the least**.
- Which car costs **the least**?

- **Enough :** sufficient in quantity or number, eg.
  - We've got **more** than **enough** but they've **hardly enough** money to spend.
  - This suit is **too expensive** but that one's **cheap enough** to buy.
  - Please tell me, is he **rich enough** to buy this grand mansion?
  - Would you be **good enough** to close the door after you?

  Enough is enough! (= stop it! I can't bear all this any more)

  Note : You say this when you want someone to stop criticizing you.

  That's enough! (= stop arguing and go away)

  That's enough! If you said any more, I'll knock out your teeth.

❑❑❑

Unit-46 Numerical Expressions (संख्यात्मक अभिव्यक्ति)

How to Say Numbers (संख्या को कैसे बोलें)

Remember : Hundred, thousand and million take 'a' or 'one' before them.

Look at the examples :

- He's earning **one** hundred rupees per day.
- I want to live for **a** hundred years.
- He has saved **one** thousand rupees.
- A million is **a** very large amount.

Note : '**a**' is informal; '**one**' is used in counting.

He ran a mile in **five** minutes, not **two**.

Similarly : **a** foot/**one** foot (**four** inches, etc.)

He returned in **an** hour/he took **one hour ten** minutes to do the job.

Remember : in spoken English saying teas, coffees, etc. is quite normal.

Look at the examples :

- Send **four** teas and a coffee, please. (One/two/three/four)
- **A** coffee means : **a** cup of coffee, **four** coffees means : '**4** cups of coffee.'
- At a restaurant, a tea stall or a coffee bar you might hear people saying :
- I've already ordered for **one** coffee and **three** teas.
- Please, send four **teas** and three **coffees** and **a** beer for Mr. Yogi.

In British English 'and' is used before the last 'two' figures :

429 as '**four** hundred **and** twenty-nine.'

(**Am Eng :** four hundred twenty nine)

Similarly : 5085 as '**five** thousand **and** eighty five.'

(**Am Eng :** five thousand eighty five)

Note : It is common to say : **eleven hundred,** etc. instead of saying : one thousand one hundred.

Say : hundred/thousand/million with a "definite number".

They are never made plural, eg : **two** hundred/**five** thousand/**ten** million, etc.

(**Don't say :** two hundreds, five thousands .... etc.)

But, it correct to say : hundreds (of), thousands (of) ....., etc.

For example : hundreds of people died/thousands **of** rupees have been wasted, etc.

- **Plural expressions with numbers, *e.g.* :**

Ten rupees/five miles, etc. is considered 'singular' when used as adjectives.

Look at the examples :

Hundred rupees	a hundred-rupee note
Three months	a three-month course
Fifteen minutes	a fifteen-minute walk
hundred metres	a hundred-metre race
Sixty years	a sixty-year old man
Five acres	a five-acre plot

A cashier at the counter.

How would you like your money? The answer could be :

"In **tens**, please" (Or) : Give me **five**, 100-rupee notes.

(**Don't say :** 100 rupees notes)

Give <u>one</u> **500 rupee**-note and <u>ten</u> **20-rupee** notes, please.

Expressing time and distance (**समय और दूरी को अभिव्यक्त करना**)

Look at these examples :

A twenty-minute taxi ride will take you to the main market.

Similarly : two hours' delay; ten days' journey; a week's holiday.

An hour's/a two-hours drive/ a ten-minutes ride, etc.

Say : It's a thirty mile drive from here to the station.

It's a short bus ride to the airport.

- **Quantities** (**मात्राएँ**) **:** (uses of fractions)

Say : 1/2 (one half); 1/4 (one-fourth/a quarter); 1/3 (one-third); 1/8 (one eight); 3/8 (three-eights); 9/16 (nine sixteenth); 2½ (two and half); 2¾ (two and three quarters) etc.

- **There are certain things which are usually bought in dozens.**

Say : Give a dozen eggs and **two** dozen oranges, please.

Give me **a** dozen rolls (= bread rolls), please.

Don't say : dozens (- s is not used with a definite number)

But : dozens of eggs were wasted/scores of people were in line, etc.

I did some shopping yesterday

I bought

Butter : five hundred grams; a loaf of bread; half a kilo of milk; two packets of coffee; a kilo of sugar; **apples :** three kilograms; half a kilo of fresh onions; a quarter of fresh **garlic**; a dozen of **eggs** and five **oranges**.

Asking and saying how much things cost :

Q. : How much is 2½ kg of potatoes? (= What's the price of ....?)

Ans : It is/It's twenty five rupees. (= it costs ......)

Q. : How much is 500 gm of sugar?

Ans : it is/It's fifteen rupees.

- **Here are some more examples :**

(a) At the grocer's :

Shopkeeper : Can I help you? (= = may I show you anything)

Krishnkant : Yes; I want some sugar.

Shopkeeper : How much do you want?

Krishnkant : Half a kilo. How much is it? (= What price is it?)

Shopkeeper : It is/It's 30 rupees per kilo.

Krishnkant : It's quite expensive. What about wheat flour?

Shopkeeper : It's twenty rupees a kilo, a little cheaper this week.

Krishnkant : But sugar is still expensive at thirty rupees a kilo.

Shopkeeper : That's right.

Krishnkant : Well anyway, pack five kg of sugar, please.

(b) At the green grocer's

Fresh green vegetables :

Potatoes/sweet potatoes/peas and green beans/cabbages/cauliflowers/ carrots/onions/green onions/garlic/ginger/lettuces/ mushrooms/ aubergines/tomatoes/radishes/pumpkins/cucumber etc.

Prices this week

New potatoes are ten rupees per kilo; carrots are 8 rupees per kilo and cabbages are cheaper at 80 np each; large cabbages are 1.50 rupees each. Home-grown vegetables are available at much cheaper rate this week. Grapes are still expensive at 45 rupees per kilo.

Conversation :

Abhaya : have you got any potatoes?

Shopkeeper : No, we haven't got new potatoes.
We've got some cabbages and good tomatoes.

Abhaya : I don't need any cabbages. how much are these potatoes?

Shopkeeper : ten rupees a kilo. how much do you want?

Abhaya : 3 kg; and a two rupees' worth of lemons, please.

Shopkeeper : Would you like some carrots?

Abhaya : No, thanks.

Unit-47 Both, all, half (of)

दोनों, सब, आधा (का)

- **Both/All :**

'Both' refers to two people, two things, two situations, etc, together.

Examples : both boys/both girls/both books/both conditions

- Hold these boxes with both hands/both her parents are sick, etc.

'All' refers to the 'whole' number of people and things.

- **Both/all (of) :**

'Both' and 'all' can be used with 'of'.

Look at the examples :

- **Both** of them are shy.
- She likes **both** of us.
- **Both** of you arrived late.
- I hate **all** of you.
- **All** of them are nice.
- **All** of us left early.

- **'All'** and **'both'** are used before 'the', 'these' and 'those', eg :
  - **All** the boys are naughty.
  - **All** these/those books are mine.
  - **Both** books are interesting.
  - **Both** the/these books are expensive.
- **'All'** and 'both' are used before possessives, eg.
  - **Both** my shirts are torn.
  - **All** his books/**all** of his books are expensive.
  - **Both** Mr Raj's daughters are intelligent.
  - **All** of his sons play well.
  - **All** Mr Raj's sons are in the army.
  - **Both** of her children go to school.
- **'Both'** and **'All'** can be used after the helping verb.

Look at the examples :

Amit and Monika were **both** absent.

(= Both Amit and Monika were absent)

Boys and girls are **all** present.

(= All the boys and girls are present)

You're **both** wrong. (= Both of you are wrong)

They've both wrong.

(= Both of them have finished the work)

- **'Both'** and **'all'** can be used before the main verb :
  - My father and mother **both** left this morning/they **all** waited for us.
  - She and her daughter **both** danced together/we all prayed for mercy.
- **'Both'** and **'all'** are placed after modals (can/could/may, etc.)

  You can **both** apply for the post/you may **all** join the party.
- **'All'** comes before numbers :

  All four girls have been selected/**all** the six terrorists surrendered last night.

  All ten passengers travelling without tickets were sent to jail.
- **Half/half** (of); **all/all** (of)

  These can be used before plural nouns, eg.
  - **Half** the eggs are fresh/**half of** the eggs are rotten. **All** children like toys.
  - **All of** the boys were punished/**all** the bread is stale/**all of** the bread is fresh.

    ('Bread' is uncountable noun here)
- **All/half** can be used with or without '<u>of</u>' before a noun :
  - **All** the country is united/**All of** the country is facing terrorism.
  - **Half** Delhi is closed/**half of** Delhi is closed because of strike.
- **'Half'** can be used before a **singular** noun :

  Say : half an hour/**half** a minute/**half** an apple.

  He gave him **half** a piece of chocolate, etc.
- **'None of'** is used as the **negative** of **'all'** eg.
  - **All** the guests arrived early. **None of** the guests arrived early.
  - **All** the hotel rooms were full. **None of** the hotel rooms were full.
- **'Neither'** is the negative of **'both'**

  Don't say : <u>Both</u> of them did not go to school.

  Say : Neither of them went to school.

Remember : 'Both' is changed into '**neither**' in the **negative**, *e.g.*

Both the girls are ugly/**neither** of the girls is ugly.

***Note :* "Neither of"** can take a singular or plural verb.

The choice depends on the context it clearly refers to.

Here are some examples :

Both of the hotels we went to were very good. **Neither** of them was/were too expensive.

Both of them can speak English fluently. But **neither** of them is/are able to speak Hindi.

I asked **both** the boys the way to the station but **neither** of them knew.

❑❑❑

Unit-48 Either/neither/also/too/as well
(या तो/नहीं/भी/भी/भी)

Either/Neither (या तो/ न तो)

- **Either :** one or the other of two (sometimes more than two)
- **'Either'** is used in front of the first of two or more alternatives.

Look at the examples :

- Ask him **either** to wait **or** go away.
- I'm expecting him **either** today **or** tomorrow.
- Here are two wrist watches – take either (= any) of them.
- You can **either** have ice cream, soup **or** fruit juice.
- Which pen shall I use? **Either**. (It doesn't matter which)
- What do you want-tea or coffee? **Either**. I don't mind.
- Come on Sunday or Monday. **Either** day is ok.
- You can have **either** this one **or** that one.

Note : verb must agree with the nearest subject, ***e.g.***

- **Either** you **or** your friends have stolen my watch.
- **Either** he or I am to go.

Look at these examples :

- **Both** the parties are claimants of this property.
- I'm ready to help if **either** of them approaches me.
- If **either** of you comes I'll help you.

Neither : not one or the other

Look at the following examples :

- We have **two** air conditioners, but **neither** is working.
- I requested **both** of them to help, but **neither** came forward.
- I'm **neither** tired **nor** hungry/he speaks **neither** Hindi nor English.
- **Both** of them were warned, but **neither** of them took it seriously.
- **Neither** of my parents is flying to New York this weekend.
- Which did you buy? **Neither**. (Neither of two was any good)
- Which one did you meet? **Neither**. (I met neither of them)
- Is your friend Hindu or Muslim? **Neither**. (He's Christian)

- What would you like-tea or coffee? **Neither**. Thanks.
- Which of those two girls is your sister? **Neither**.

Also/too/as well

The above adverbs provide some more information about a person or thing; they are similar in meaning except that **'also'** is a bit formal.

'Too' and **'as well'** are informally used in spoken English.

Look at the examples :

- Mr Sinha is our teacher. He is **also** the dean of the arts faculty.
- His son is a famous surgeon. he's **also** an excellent guitarist.
- We're thinking to invite Mr Robinson and his parents **as well**.
- She's an expert cook, a brilliant dancer and a politician, **too**.
- Where are you from? Delhi. **Me too!** I'm going to London.
- Mr Raj's daughter can sing and dance **as well**. Can you?

■ Not .... either

In negative expressions 'not...either' is used, *e.g. :*

- Does he drink ? No, and he doesn't smoke **either**.
- I **don't** like him. (**Don't say :** I also don't like him)
- I don't like him **either**. (= I don't **either**)

Similarly :

- He didn't go to school. His sister didn't (go) **either**.
- He can't swim. Can you? No, I can't **either**.
- I haven't got any money. Have you? No, I haven't **either**.

■ Patterns showing agreement and disagreement

Consider the following

(a) So + auxiliary verb + noun/pronoun

This expression is used to express agreement, *e.g. :*

- I have/I've finished my work. **So have I** (= I've finished my work, too)
- He has/He's got a car. **So has Monika**. (Monika's got a car, too/as well)
- She went to the temple. **So did her brother**. (= Her brother, too)

(b) Neither + auxiliary verb + noun/pronoun

This construction is used to express disagreement. *e.g. :*

Amit : I haven't finished my work **yet**. (= so far)

Soni : Neither have I (= I haven't either)

(or) : **Nor** have I.

Below are given some more examples :

He hasn't got a car. **Neither** has Soni. (= Soni hasn't **either**)

(or) : Nor has Soni.

I don't normally drink at dinner. **Neither** do I (= I don't **either**)

(or) : **Nor** do I.

I haven't got money. **Neither** have I (= I haven't **either**)

(or) : **Nor** have I.

I can't swim. **Neither** can I (= I can't **either**)

(or) : **Nor** can I.

They didn't like the film. **Neither** did we (= we didn't **either**)

(or) : **Nor** did we

The boys weren't well dressed.

Neither were girls. (= The girls weren't **either**)

(or) : **Nor** were girls

❑❑❑

Unit-49 Wishes and Regrets

(शुभकामनाएँ और पछतावा)

Expressing Wishes (इच्छा व्यक्त करना)

When you say, "I want to go" you are expressing a desire in the present. The same can be expressed in a formal style : "I wish to go". Sometimes your wish could be unreal, that is, very unlikely to come true; for example, when you say, "I wish to be a millionaire" your desire is for something impossible. how to express the imposible or unreal in the present is what you are going to learn in this unit.

- **Expressing 'unreal' in the present** (वर्तमान में कल्पना व्यक्त करना)

  Consider the following sentence :

  "I wish I were a millionaire!"

  In the above sentence the **verb** is in the **past** with a **present** meaning. Remember : Statements expressing **unreal** or **wished for** (now), take **past form** of the **verb**.

  The **Past** used in this way refers to **present,** and not the **past time.**

- **The use of 'were'**

  'Were' is formally used in imaginary used in imaginary statements and is prefereble to 'was'. Some people consider the use of '**were**' more correct. Below are given a few examples.

  The '**past**' is used in these sentences refers to **present** or **future :**

  - I wish **I were** a bird! (A desire for impossible)
  - I wish **I were** dead!
  - If she **were** my wife!
  - If only my father **were** here!
  - If only **I had** a scooter!
  - If only **I knew** the answer!
  - I wish **I knew** the secret!
  - If only she **could** see her son now.

  Note : 'If only' usually expresses a strong desire or regret.

- **The use of 'wish/if only' with the past continuous, *e.g.* :**
  - I **wish** a lot of flowers **were** blooming in my garden!
  - If **only** you and me **were** travelling around the world!

▪ Consider the following expressions :

It is (high) time; as if

Compare It's time for us to go. (It's the proper time)
It's time we **went**. (We're already late)
It's time the children **were** in bed. (They're late)
It's **high** time we **went**. (Emphatic : It's too late)

Compare It's time for you to work hard. (The proper time has arrived)
It's time you **started** working hard. (You're already late)

Compare He walks **as if** he's lame. (Seems to be lame)
He walks **as if** he **were** lame. (He's acting as lame)
He walks **as if** he **knew** everything. (To impress others)
He orders me **as if I were** his subordinate. (But I am not)

▪ Suppose/supposing (मान लीजिए) (= What would happen if ....?)

Expressing impatience/doubt/possibility, etc. in the present/future

Look at the examples :

- Suppose they **arrived** late!
- Suppose your father **saw** you with me!
- Suppose she **fell** in love with her boss!
- Supposing they **met** with an accident!
- Supposing your prediction **went** wrong!

▪ Expressing unreal in the past (भूत में कल्पना व्यक्त करना)

'Past perfect' should be used to express a desire or wish in the past. Look at the following examples :

Now	**In the past**
I wish **I were** on the site of accident!	I wish I'd (= I had) been on the site of accident
If only you **didn't eat** so much!	If only you **hadn't eaten** so much!
If only **I knew** him earlier!	If only I'd (= I had) known him earlier!
I wish you **were** my teacher!	I wish you'd (= you had) been my teacher!

□□□

Unit-50 Conditional Sentence
(सशर्त वाक्य)

- A conditional sentence beginning with 'if' or 'unless' deals with possibilities and probabilities.

Look at the following example :

Tanya : It's cloudy today. Will it rain?

Prakash : It's **possible** but not **probable** before evening.

The sentence, "It is cloudy today" expresses the **possibility** of rain. Amit admits the **possibility** but does not consider it **probable** (= likely to be true) before evening. Now consider this sentence :

"**If it rains,** I will not go out"

These clause, "If it rains" in the sentence above introduces a condition.

Remember : A conditional clause usually begins with "if" though other conjunctions can also be used instead.

Conditionals are of three basic types :

If you want to say that something 'will happen' or probably won't happen.

Type 1 : (If + present) + Future should be used.

Remember sentence of this type refer to the **present** or **future,** for example :

- **If he comes**, I will help him/I'll help him **if he comes**.
- **If he doesn't hurry**, he'll be late/he'll be late **if he doesn't hurry**.

Note : The use of 'present' in the "if clauses" suggests that the action is possible.

Look at these examples :

- If he **arrives** late, we **won't** be able to catch the plane.
- If she **finishes** work early, she**'ll go** home.
- What **will happen** if you **miss** the train?
- If **I miss** the train, **I'll stay** at home.
- If you **drive fast**, you**'ll** soon **get** there.
- What **will** you **say** if you **meet** him?
- You**'ll be** late if you **don't leave** now.
- **unless** you leave now, you**'ll be** late.

Note : the 'if-clause' may be in the first place or may follow the main clause.

- **Remember : All present tenses are possible after "if" in type (1)**

Similarly : other future tenses can also be used in the main clause.

Look at the examples :

- If she **stays** in Agra till May, she**'ll have been living** here for 20 years.
- If they**'ve arrived** at the airport, they**'ll be** here by seven o'clock.
- If they**'ve been dancing** all night, they**'ll get tired** more than others.
- If **I'm feeling** better tomorrow, **I'll eat** some food.
- If the weather**'s** fine, we**'ll go** for a picnic.
- She**'ll be** very angry if you **break** any more plates.
- I can **give** you an apple if you **keep** your mouth shut.

- **Look at these conjunctions :**

Unless. provided, on the condition, Suppose/supposing

Unless : If ..... not

Unless you (= if you don't)

There are some examples :

- **Unless** you work hard, you **can't pass** the exam.
- **Unless** we **have** rain soon, there **will be** a famine.
- **Unless** you hurry, you**'ll be** late.
- **Provided :** on the condition (that)
- We**'ll go** provided (that) the weather**'s** fine.
- We**'ll go** on the condition (that) the weather**'s** fine.
- **Suppose/supposing : "What if ?"** (= asking about the consequences)
- Suppose/supposing the police arrive, what will happen to us?
- Suppose/supposing the train is late, where will we stay?
- Suppose/supposing something goes wrong, what will you do then?

- **The use of 'should' makes the condition more polite**

Look at the examples :

- Should you meet him, ask him to ring me. (= If you ....)
- Should she calls, tell her I'll ring back. (=If she ....)
- Should you see Mr Raman, please give him my regards.
- Should you happen to see Neha say, I'm coming next week.
- Should anyone happen to come, say : I'll be back by ten.

- **Uses of modals in the main clause :**

- If you finish your work early, **you can/may/must phone me**.

- If the weather's fine tomorrow, we **might** go out.
- If it's too hot this evening, he **oughtn't** to come here.

■ Type 2 : (If + past) + would

'Type two' also refers to the present or future, but with a difference. The **'Past'** in the **'if-clause'** makes the action **uncertain** (doubtful).

Look at the example :

- If it **'rained'** I would not go out

Note : the speaker in the above example does not expect it will rain.

'Would' is normally used with **all** persons in the **main** clause but **'should'** can **replace** it in the **first** person.

'Contracted forms' are commonly used in everyday speech, *e.g.*

I'd (I would); **we'd** (= we would); **you'd** (= you would); **he'd** (= he would); **she'd** (= she would); **they'd** (= they would), etc.

Compare :

Type-1	**Type-2**
Suggests possibility, *e.g.* :	Suggests uncertainty. (doubt), *e.g.*
If you fly by plane, you**'ll get** earlier.	If you **flew** by plane, you**'d get** earlier.
If he **comes, I'll help** him.	If he **came, I'd help** him.
You**'ll get** wet if it **rains**.	You**'d get** wet if it **rained**.

■ Type 3 : (It did not happen) :
(If + past perfect) + would have + past participle

This type suggests that the action did not happen in the past.

Contracted forms are commonly used in conversation :

I'd (= I had/woud); **we'd** (= we had/woud); **you'd** (= you had/woud); **He'd** (= he had/woud); **she'd** (= she had/woud); **they'd** (= they had/woud)

Note : the sort form **would've** (= would have) is common in speech.

Say : 'could have' as **could've** in conversation.

Examples :

- If he'd tried, he would've succeeded.
- If he hadn't tried, he wouldn't have succeeded.

Note : Could/might/should + have can be used in the main clause.

(a) **(Type 3) :** suggests the action did not happen, eg :

- If **I'd** (= I had) **bought** a car, **I would've taken** you to Delhi in it.

- I **shouldn't have eaten** it, if **I'd** (= I had) **known** that there was garlic in it.
- If it **had been raining** this morning, I **would've stayed** at home.
- If you'**d** (= you had) **been** here yesterday, **I might have told** you the truth.
- If you **hadn't worked** hard at university, you **wouldn't have gotten** a better job.

(b) Talking about imaginary situation :(Type 3)

- If the driver **had been** careless (but was not), all the passengers **would've died/been dead** (but it didn't happen)
- If he **hadn't been wearing** the bulletproof jacket, he **would've died**.
- What **would've happened** if you **hadn't been wearing** your helmet?
- If I **hadn't been wearing** my helmet, I **would've met** with an accident.
- If **I'd got** a lot of money, life **would've been operating** on patients.
- If **I'd** (= I had) **been** a surgeon, **I would've been operating** on patients.
- If **I'd** (= I had) **been** you, **I would've rejected** the marriage proposal.

Note : 'had been' can combine with noun/adjective/state/mood, etc.

❑❑❑